COMPUSERVE UK
in easy steps

Dave Howell

COMPUTER
STEP

In easy steps is an imprint of Computer Step
Southfield Road . Southam
Warwickshire CV33 OFB . England

Tel: 01926 817999 Fax: 01926 817005
http://www.computerstep.com

Notice of Liability
Every effort has been made to ensure that this book contains accurate and current information. However, Computer Step and the author shall not be liable for any loss or damage suffered by readers as a result of any information contained herein.

Trademarks
All trademarks are acknowledged as belonging to their respective companies.

Printed and bound in the United Kingdom

ISBN 1-874029-33-4

Contents

5   Chat   99

6   Forums   113

7   Communities   123

8   Your Personal Home Page   175

Index   189

Installing CompuServe

In this chapter you will learn how to install the software that will allow you to access CompuServe.

Chapter One

Covers

Introduction

CompuServe Interactive (CSi) is the world's largest Internet service provider. It has approximately 5 million members worldwide, with 400,000 of these based in the UK. The service splits between CSi and CNS (CompuServe Network Services). CNS provides the connections or bandwidth to companies who want to connect to the Internet. However, the public only sees CSi, as this is where the Internet services are based. CSi does however offer more than a simple connection to the Internet. On its servers you will find content that you have access to either free of charge as part of your membership, or with the payment of a premium. From travel to education, CSi contains information that you can gain access to.

The vast majority of people want to use their Internet connection for e-mail. This is the single most common use of a connection at this time. CSi provides this service, allowing members to send messages to anyone in the world with an e-mail address.

Unique to CSi are the Forums. These are specific areas of the system where people can meet and discuss a wide range of subjects. At the present time there are over 1,600 Forums. Also, many of the largest companies have specific Forums on CSi. If you need technical assistance, you may be able to ask the company directly through their own unique Forum.

At the time of writing, existing users will know that CSi is changing its design. Many of the services that are available are being given a completely new look. CSi is creating 21 Communities grouped into 7 categories, which include: Computing, News, Business & Professional, Leisure, Recreation, Reference and Education.

Installing CompuServe

HANDY TIP

If you are using your PC in its standard mode, you will probably have a screen resolution of 800 x 600 pixels. This is more than adequate for the setup procedure. You can increase this by right-clicking on your desktop, selecting Properties from the pop-up menu, and then selecting the Settings tab.

After you have inserted the CompuServe CD-ROM into your CD-ROM drive, the CompuServe interactive tour should start automatically (if you don't have AutoPlay turned on, you may need to run the tour manually using Windows Explorer). If you haven't seen this before, or would like to know more about the services that are on offer, sit back and enjoy the show. At any time, you can end this multimedia tour and go to the sign-up procedure by clicking on the box that appears on the screen. You will also see a dialogue informing you that you may need to change your screen settings to see the tour in its best resolution.

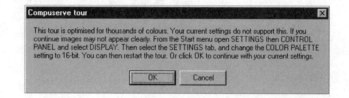

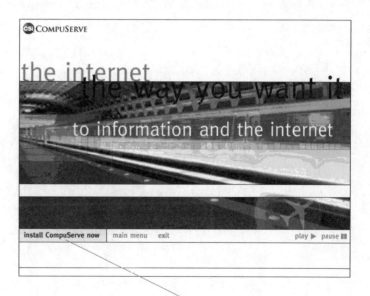

Click here to start the sign-up process at any time during the tour.

When you exit the tour to begin your first sign-up session, this dialogue box will appear.

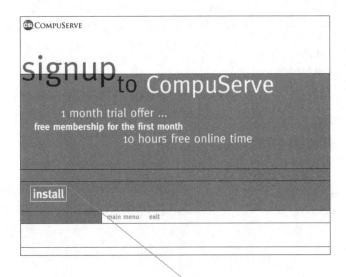

| Click on the Install button to start the sign-up Wizard.

2 Windows will now spring into action by starting the InstallShield Wizard.

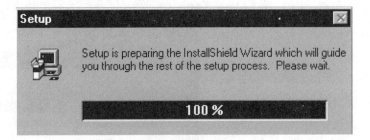

You will now see the first screen of the Installation Wizard that you will have seen when you have installed other software on your computer.

3 In most cases you will leave this screen as it appears. However, if your PC is connected to a network of some kind, choose this option. You will then be taken to another set of screens. In this case we will follow the setup for a stand-alone PC. Click on Next to move to the next screen.

REMEMBER **If you know that your computer is on a network, check with your administrator before you install the CSi software**

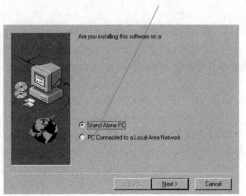

4 Here you choose the kind of installation you want from the CD-ROM. In most circumstances the first button should be pressed. This is the fastest means of getting the CompuServe software onto your system. If, however, you encounter some problems with the installation, you have the option of using the 'Custom' button. This allows you to choose which parts of the CompuServe software are installed and in which areas on your hard drive.

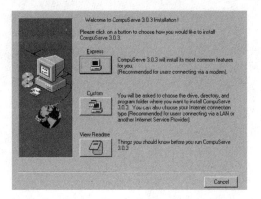

5 When you see this dialogue box, click on OK to restart your computer.

HANDY TIP

The installation process may have added some components to your operating system that won't become active until you reboot your PC. If you try and access CSi without restarting your PC you may have problems connecting.

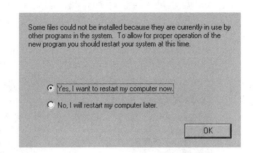

Some files could not be installed because they are currently in use by other programs in the system. To allow for proper operation of the new program you should restart your system at this time.

◉ Yes, I want to restart my computer now.

○ No, I will restart my computer later.

OK

6 When your computer has shut down and Windows has restarted, it will take a moment to update your shortcuts and your desktop. You should see a new CompuServe icon on your desktop. Also check that the CSi button has been added to your Start menu.

These two entries should now appear on your desktop. You can start the CompuServe software by clicking on either of these.

7 The installation procedure is in two parts. Once the files you need have been copied across to your hard drive, you will see this Welcome screen. This is when you will complete the sign-up section of the installation. Click on the Signup button.

8 This is the first screen of the Installation Wizard. Click on Next.

9 Choose United Kingdom from the countries listed: this will allow you to gain access to CompuServe with the correct telephone number. Then click Next.

HANDY TIP

CompuServe has recently set up a single access number for the whole of the UK: 0845 080 1000.

10 For the moment, choose the best access number from the list in this dialogue box. When you have fully installed your software you can change this again to one more suitable. Click Next when you have finished.

11 Carefully look through this list of settings. If any of them apply to the type of connection you have, put a tick in the box next to the entry. Then click Next.

12 Activate the port that you are using here. If you are unsure, select Auto-Detect. Click Next when you have finished.

13 If you asked the software to auto-detect which modem port you are using, you will see this dialogue box. Click Next to continue.

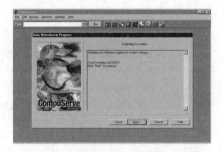

If the access phone number that appears in the window here isn't the correct one to access the CSi service, you have a chance to change this now. Click on the Modify Phone Number button to do this before proceeding.

14 This is the last section of this part of the sign-up procedure. If you want to check anything that you have entered, click on the Back button. You can also modify the phone number you have chosen if you need to. When you are happy with the settings, click Finish.

15 The CompuServe software will now dial out to continue with the sign-up procedure. You should see this dialogue box to tell you what your PC is doing.

...contd

16 Choose the best contact number that matches the speed of your modem. When you have chosen a telephone number, click on Next.

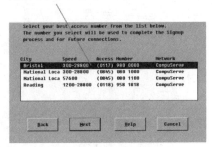

17 As the dialogue box states, you may have to modify this number. For now, however, just click on Next to move to the next screen.

18 This is the next dialogue box that you see. The CompuServe software will connect you to the service with the number you have selected.

...contd

 HANDY TIP

If you cannot locate your offer code, you can still access CompuServe by typing NEWMEMBER in the box.

19 If you got your CD as a magazine cover disk, you should have a code, which you should now type into this box. When you have entered it, click Next.

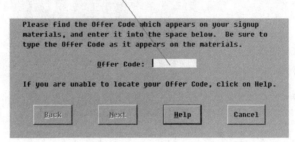

Please find the Offer Code which appears on your signup materials, and enter it into the space below. Be sure to type the Offer Code as it appears on the materials.

Offer Code:

If you are unable to locate your Offer Code, click on Help.

Back   Next   Help   Cancel

20 Enter all of the information that this dialogue box asks for, then click Next.

First Name:
Last Name:
House # and Street Name:
Town/City:
Postcode:
Evening Phone Number:
Daytime Phone Number:

Back   Next   Help   Cancel

21 Choose your method of payment and click Next.

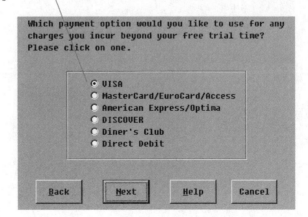

Which payment option would you like to use for any charges you incur beyond your free trial time? Please click on one.

- VISA
- MasterCard/EuroCard/Access
- American Express/Optima
- DISCOVER
- Diner's Club
- Direct Debit

Back   Next   Help   Cancel

22 Select which mailing lists and directories you wish your name to be included in. When you have, click Next.

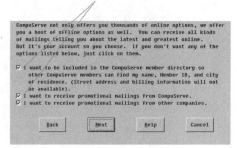

23 When you click on Next on the last dialogue box, the CompuServe software will begin to process your details. You should see this dialogue box on your screen when this is happening.

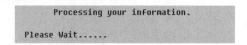

24 This dialogue box provides some useful information about your free hours on CompuServe. Scroll down the window by using the down arrow on the right of the window. When you have finished, click Next to move on.

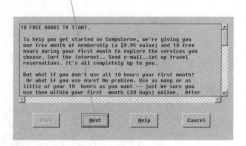

...contd

25 This is your user agreement. Read it carefully. If you are happy with the terms and conditions of the agreement, put a tick in the 'Agree' box and click Next to move to the next screen.

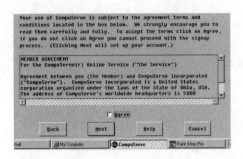

26 On this screen you should now see your new membership number and password. Keep these in a safe place, as you will need them to access your account. Click Next to move on.

 When you are confirming your password and ID number, pay special attention when you type it in to get it exactly right. Pay close attention to any special characters that are in your password. You must type these exactly as you see them.

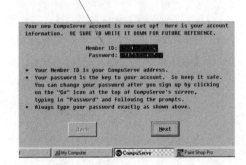

27 CompuServe will then ask you to confirm your member ID and password. Click Next when you have typed in this information.

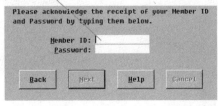

28 This is your final screen. It confirms that your software has
installed correctly and that you have given CompuServe all
the information it needs to set up your account. Click OK.

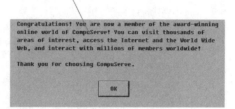

This is the main screen of the CompuServe software. From
here you navigate the service. You can change the settings
that you have entered into the software, for instance, and
also correct any errors that might have occurred in the
installation if you find you are not able to connect to
CompuServe when you try for the first time.

Try connecting to CompuServe
now by clicking on this icon.

29 When you click on the Connect icon, you should see this dialogue box. It will keep you informed about how your connection is proceeding.

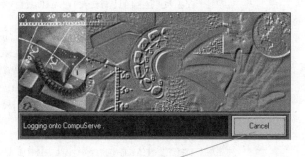

Logging onto CompuServe . | Cancel |

You can cancel the connection at any time by clicking on this button.

If all goes well, you will be connected to CSi, with the main screen displayed. From here you can move to the various areas of CSi, such as Mail, Forums or Chat. If you are not connected to the CSi service, read the 'Troubleshooting Overview' topic in Chapter Two. Here you will find advice on checking your settings and fixing any problems you may have.

If your computer dials out and connects to the CSi server but seems to stop for a long time without logging you onto the system, you may have some problems with your connection. There are a number of areas that you should look at first before trying to connect again.

Modem
Check that you have your modem plugged in and set up correctly. If you have been using it for another service, try switching it off and back on again. This should reset it. Try and connect again.

Check that you have the correct driver for your modem selected. If you don't, you will need to set this up through the Control Panel. Click on Start>Settings>Control Panel, then double click on the Modems icon and follow the Setup Wizard to install the correct driver for your modem.

Dial-Up Networking

The new CSi software uses this section of the Windows operating system. Dial-Up Networking sets up a connection for the CSi software to use when you are accessing its services, and also uses this connection when you are looking at Web pages.

You must make sure that all of the components of Dial-Up Networking have been correctly installed on your PC. This will then set up the correct TCP/IP setting and the Dial-Up Adapter. With these correctly installed you should then be able to connect to the CSi service.

Consult your Windows manual or on-line help to install the correct modem driver and all the components of Dial-Up Networking.

Setting Preferences

CSi needs to be set up so that it works with a number of elements of the CSi service and the Windows operating system. In this chapter you can check that you have the correct settings entered in the software and also find help with any problems you may have connecting.

Chapter Two

Covers

Introduction

The CSi software, when it is installed, should set itself up so that you can log onto the service without any problems. It is, however, possible that the installation may need some help with the settings or preferences side of the setup procedure. Every user's system is set up differently. As the CSi software connects to a number of areas of your system, it is inevitable that some conflicts may occur

In this chapter you will find details of how your preferences should be set up. In the vast majority of cases, this will solve any problems you may have with connecting to the CSi service.

However, if you are still have problems after working through this chapter, please refer to the Troubleshooting Overview topic on page 37 for further information.

The Connection Tab

1 From the CSi main screen, select the Access menu and click on the Preferences entry.

2 This is the main Preferences screen. From here you can input all of the settings that CSi expects when it starts. If any of these are incorrect, the software will not be able to connect to the service.

HANDY TIP

If you encounter general connection problems, always double-check that you have everything set correctly in this dialogue box first, before looking elsewhere to solve the problem.

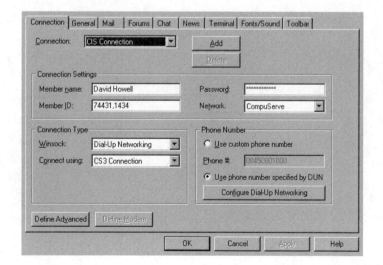

3 On the main screen, check that the following are correct:

Connection
CIS Connection

Check carefully that these are entered correctly.

Member Name
Member ID
Password

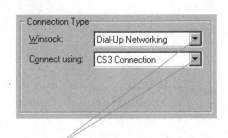

Winsock
Dial-Up Networking.

Connect Using
CS3 Connection.

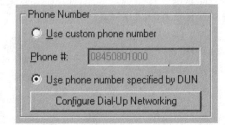

Use the down arrows to select the correct entries if they do not appear in the boxes.

Phone Number
Make sure that the 'Use phone number specified by DUN' option is activated.

...contd

4 Now click on Configure
Dial-Up Networking.
The following dialogue
box appears.

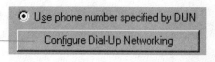

**CompuServe
has
recently
set up a
single access
number for the
whole of the UK:
0845 080 1000.**

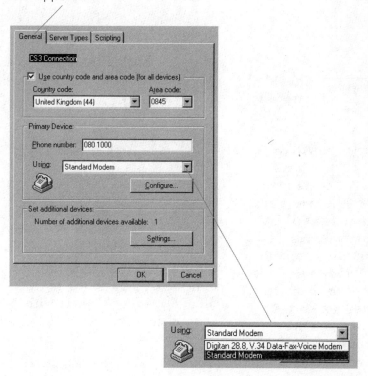

Check that all of the settings appear as they do here. If
your modem does not appear in the 'Using' box, you will
need to select this by clicking on the down arrow. If your
modem does not appear in the list, you will have to install
it. See page 52 for how to do this.

5 Click on the Configure button to check that you have set up the modem correctly. The following dialogue box appears.

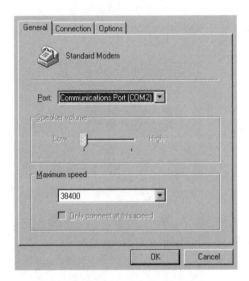

All of these parameters were set when the CSi software was installed on your PC. However, it is best to check that they are correct when you are troubleshooting any connection problems.

Here you can see the COM port to which your modem is connected, and also the maximum speed that your modem will allow you to connect with. When you have checked these, click on the Connection tab.

6 Click on the Connection tab to check your connection preferences. They should be set as they are here. Click OK.

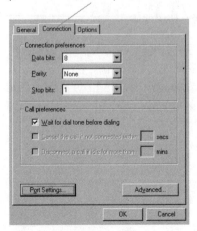

...contd

HANDY TIP

If you don't have TCP/IP as an option to put a tick by, you have not installed this as a component of Windows. Select Start>Settings> Control Panel, then double-click on the Modems icon and install TCP/IP and the Dial-Up Adapter now.

7 Clicking on the Server Types tab will open this dialogue box. Check that the Type of Dial-Up Server has the CISPPP:PPP entry highlighted. If it is not, click the down arrow. If you do not have this entry at all to choose when you click the down arrow, choose the PPP: Windows 95 entry, as you see here. Also check that you only have these two entries ticked.

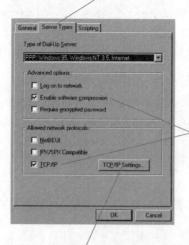

8 Click on the TCP/IP Settings button. If you are having problems connecting to CSi, and this dialogue box is greyed out, try entering the Primary and Secondary numbers as you see below. This may correct the problem. When you have finished, click OK.

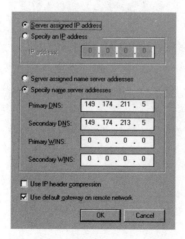

2 Setting Preferences **29**

...contd

 In the vast majority of cases the CISPPP server will automatically be installed on your PC. If this is the case then you won't see this dialogue box at all. It is only for PPP:Windows 95 server users.

9 To log onto CSi, a special script is run. This holds all of the settings that CSi needs to connect you to the service. Some users may have problems if their systems did not install the CIS server when they first installed the CompuServe software. Click on the Scripting tab and check if a script is listed. If there is one then you probably only have the PPP server installed. You checked this in step 7 on page 29.

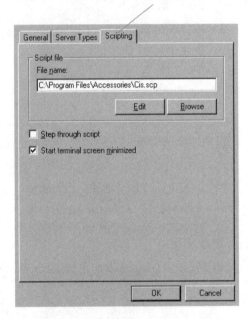

10 When you have checked this dialogue box, click OK and return to the main Preferences screen.

Accessing the Internet

When you install the CSi software for the first time off the CD-ROM, you will be asked if you want to install Internet Explorer if this isn't already on your system. CSi provides what is called a gateway to the Internet. As well as the other services that CSi offers to its members such as email and the new communities, you can also surf the Internet. You access this through the main CSi software by clicking on the 'Browse the Internet' icon in the tool bar.

Browse the Internet

To do this you need to set up the Internet browser that CSi will use when you click on this icon. You can also go straight to a World-Wide Web page by putting its address into the box on the main CSi screen.

 When you are entering addresses for Web pages, take care to get the address exactly right. If special characters are used, make sure they are also entered correctly. If not, your browser will not be able to find the Web site.

You can also save yourself the time of typing in an address. If you click on the down arrow, you can select a Web site or an area of the CSi service you have recently visited.

If you look at the main screen area of the CSi software, you will see that it has an Internet button. This is the third way that you can start your browser and look at Web pages.

Internet

REMEMBER

You have a choice of how your Internet browser is used within the CSi software. This is covered in the next chapter.

Once you have started your Internet browser, you will not have to return to this screen each time you want to move to a different Web site. When the browser has started it takes over from the CSi software until you have finished looking at your Web sites.

Setting Up Your Internet Browser

You can make any Web browser you like your default by following these steps.

1 Start the CSi software, drop down the Access menu and click on Preferences.

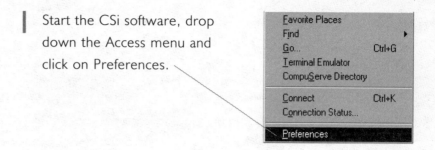

2 The Preferences dialogue will open. Click on the General tab.

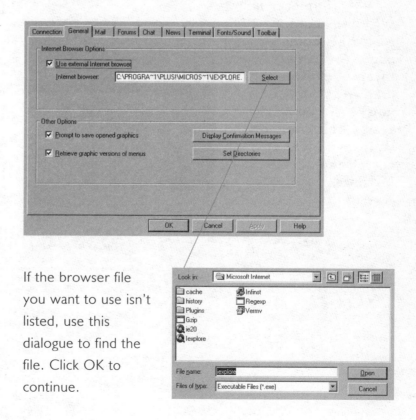

If the browser file you want to use isn't listed, use this dialogue to find the file. Click OK to continue.

3 In the General tab, put a tick next to the 'Use external Internet browser' option and use the Select button to set the path to your chosen browser – in this case, Internet Explorer. Click OK when you have finished to return to the main Preferences screen, and then OK again to move back to the CSi main screen.

4 You should now have your Internet browser set up. When you have successfully connected to the CSi service, click on the Internet icon, or enter a Web address. In this case, the browser that has been set up is the one supplied with the CSi software. You should see its main screen open and its default start page displayed.

HANDY TIP

At the moment, Internet Explorer is set up to load the Microsoft home page. You can set Internet Explorer to load any Web site you like when it starts. This could be your favourite search engine, for instance.

5 You also have the option of running your Web browser internally within the CSi software. In this way, you will always have the same screen open on your monitor and will therefore be able to switch between Web sites and CSi services. At the moment there is a split between those services that are available through CSi itself, and those available on the CSi Web site.

HANDY TIP

If you decide to view Web sites internally to the CSi software, you will not have as much control over the information that the site has to offer. If you want to save a page or a section of a Web site, you can only do this if you have the Web site loaded into an external browser.

Eventually all of CSi's services will move to the Internet. In the meantime you have a choice of how you view your CSi information and the Web sites you visit. Many users set up their CSi software so it runs their Web browser externally. This way they know when they are accessing the Internet and when they are using the CSi services such as the Communities.

If you want to view your Web sites internally within the CSi software, make sure that the check box in the dialogue box that is shown in step 2 is not ticked. You will then see Web sites displayed in your CSi software, with the CSi task bar still in place – as you can see in the screenshot below.

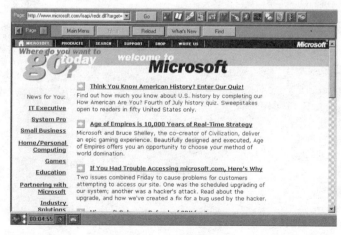

6 As you are now using your Web browser internally, you will see a new button appear in the dialogue box that you opened in step 2.

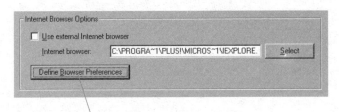

Click on this Define Browser Preferences button now to open the following dialogue box:

7 When you have checked your settings, click OK to return to the main CSi menu screen.

Click on the Connection tab and check that the connection type is set to 'CS3 Connection'.

Troubleshooting Overview

HANDY TIP

There is a file that you can download from the CSi service that has more information on troubleshooting. In the UK Help Forum, look for the file CS303.DOC.

In the rest of this chapter you will find information that will help you solve some of the main problems you may encounter when you install the CSi software and try to make a connection. Some of the bug fixes that you will see details of here, however, need you to download a small patch program from the CSi service itself. You will therefore have to get your connection working before you can get hold of these programs and upgrade your software.

Many of the problems that users face can usually be dealt with by taking a close look at how the preferences have been set up when the CSi software was installed. You can check how they should be set up by looking at the topic 'The Connection Tab' earlier in this chapter. Here you will see how your preferences should be set up. Check each one carefully.

HANDY TIP

CSi also have a small utility program that is available on-line. This automatically detects any problems by looking at your system and reporting any problems. In the UK Help Forum, look for the file CSIDIAG.EXE.

If you still have problems connecting to CSi then the rest of this chapter should help you solve the majority of your problems. If not, you can contact the CompuServe technical help line on 0990 000 100.

Installing Dial-Up Networking

The CSi software takes advantage of a section of the Windows operating system called Dial-Up Networking. Depending on how you have your PC set up, you may or may not have this installed on your machine. Without this Windows component, you will not be able to connect to CSi no matter what you do, as this software is what makes the connection when you log on.

Here's how to check that you have Dial-Up Networking installed on your system. If you don't have it installed, you'll learn here how to install it now.

HANDY TIP

You can also check Dial-Up Networking by opening the My Computer icon, and then the Dial-Up Networking folder.

A fast way to check if you have Dial-Up Networking installed on your system is to check through the Start menu. Click on the Start button now.

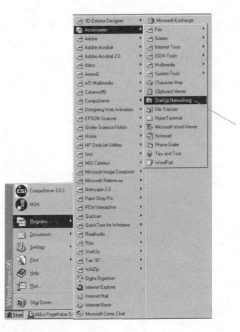

2 Move your mouse to the Programs entry on the menu that appears and then up to Accessories. Another menu will appear. You should see an entry for Dial-Up Networking.

...contd

3 If you do not see this entry, you don't currently have Dial-Up Networking installed. You must now install this component of the Windows operating system before proceeding any further. The files that you will need will be on your Windows CD-ROM.

Installing Dial-Up Networking

Click on the Start button, then move up to the Settings entry on the menu. You will see another menu appear. Click on the Control Panel entry.

...contd

Add/Remove
Programs

2 When the Control Panel has opened, click on the icon labelled Add/ Remove Programs.

3 You will see this dialogue box open, listing all of the programs that are currently installed on your PC. You may be familiar with this dialogue box already, as many programs use it when they are installed on your system. Here, we are interested in the Windows components you have installed, so click on the Windows Setup tab.

Some programs use their own installation utility, but on the whole this component of Windows is usually used to add or remove programs from your PC.

HANDY TIP

You will only see these buttons if you have the WinDelete software installed.

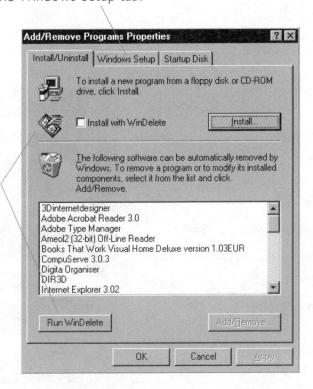

4 In the Windows Setup tab, you can see the components of the Windows operating system. A tick in the box next to each entry indicates if the component is installed or not.

This keeps track of the total amount of hard drive memory you will need to install all of the components you have selected.

5 Locate the Communications entry in the window. Highlight it and then click on the Details button.

6 Here you can see which communication components you have installed. If a tick does not appear next to the Dial-Up Networking and Phone Dialler, click on the boxes to their left to put a tick next to them.

A description of each component will appear in this box as you click on each one in the main window.

After you have selected the components and installed them onto your system, you will be asked if you want to restart your PC. Do this now and then check through the Start button and the Accessories entry to see if Dial-Up Networking has now been successfully installed. Try to connect to CSi again.

Checking Your CS3 Connection

One of the error messages that you may see concerns the CS3 connection that you need to set up within the Dial-Up Networking component. The CS3 connection is where you give Dial-Up Networking a specific set of instructions and details about the kind of connection you want to make. In some cases this connection will need to be recreated if it has been corrupted.

1 Click on the Start button, then choose Programs>Accessories>Dial-Up Networking. Alternatively, double-click on the My Computer icon on your Windows desktop and open the Dial-Up Networking folder.

Dial-Up Networking

HANDY TIP

You can use the Preferences dialogue box to check if a CS3 connection was created when you installed the CSi software. This was covered on page 26.

2 You will see this window open when you click on the Dial-Up Networking entry in the menu. From here you can check your CS3 connection settings and create a new one if you need to.

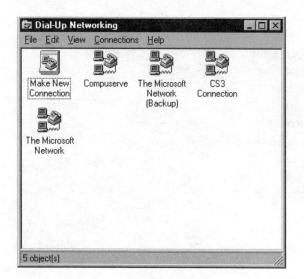

3 If you see a CS3 icon in the window that you have just opened, you can check how it has been configured by right-clicking on the icon. Do that now.

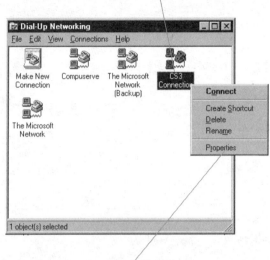

4 When this menu has popped up, move your mouse down the list until you come to the Properties entry. Click on this to open the CS3 Connection dialogue box.

HANDY TIP

When you enter the main body of the CSi telephone number, make sure you leave a space between the 080 and 1000 sections of the number.

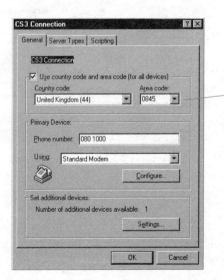

5 From this dialogue box you can now check all of the settings of the existing CS3 connection.

...contd

If you are having problems connecting to CSI, you can try to connect by changing the way that the telephone number is entered into the CS3 Connection dialogue box. Take the tick out of the 'Use Country Code and Area Code' box, and put all of the CSi telephone number – including the area code (0845) – in the box in the Primary Devices area of this dialogue box. This may correct your problem and allow you to connect to CSi.

6 Check that you have entered the correct telephone number in the General tab, and that your modem is selected. If it isn't, use the down arrow to select your modem. If it doesn't appear, see page 52 on installing your modem.

7 In the General tab, click on the Configure button to reveal the Standard Modem Properties dialogue box.

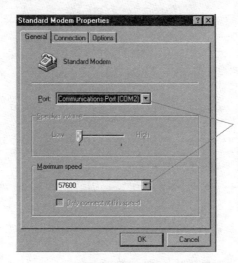

Check that the COM port is correct and that you have the maximum speed of your modem set.

8 Click on the Connection tab and check that the settings are as you see here.

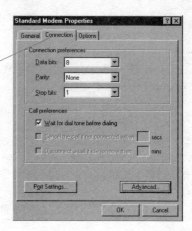

9 Click OK to move back to the first screen, as you see in step 5. Now click on the Server Types tab. In the main window you should see the server type selected. If the CSi software has installed correctly this should be the CISPPP:PPP server. If it is not visible, click the down

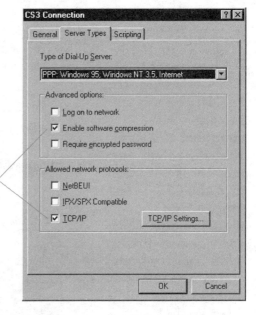

arrow and make it the active server type now. You should also check that the two entries you see here are ticked, and nothing else. Click OK when you have finished.

Make sure that you have the 'Server assigned IP address' entry activated. CSi assigns this address dynamically each time you log on. Do not enter a number in the IP address box.

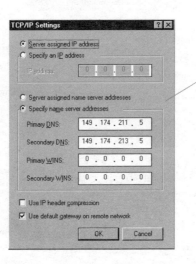

10 Click on the TCP/IP Settings button to open this dialogue box.

In some cases you can correct a connection fault by entering the Primary and Secondary DNS numbers in the TCP/IP Settings dialogue box. If you have tried unsuccessfully to connect to CSi, enter the numbers exactly as you see them in step 10.

| | The last dialogue box to check is the last tab on this screen. Click on the Scripting tab now. If you only have the PPP: Windows 95 server type on your system, you will need to check that this script is run when you attempt to log on. If you do have the CISPPP server available on your system then you will not need to check this entry. This only applies to the PPP: Windows 95 server type.

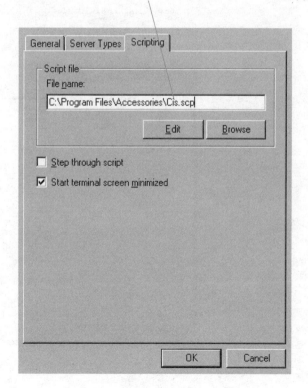

Creating a New CS3 Connection

One of the most common error messages that you may come across is concerned with the CS3 connection that was created when you installed the CSi software. In some cases this can be corrupt. To correct this fault, you will have to create a new CS3 connection.

1 Open the Dial-Up Networking folder from the My Computer icon on your Windows desktop or through the Start menu.

Dial-Up Networking

2 You will see this window open. You need to delete the existing CS3 Connection icon. Right click on it. In the pop-up menu, click on Delete.

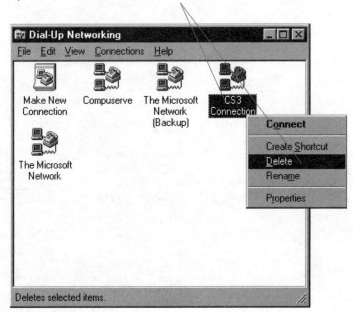

...contd

The CS3 connection is the bridge between the CSi software and the Dial-Up Networking component of Windows that makes the connection between your computer and the CSi service. Check that Dial-Up Networking is set up correctly before you create a new CS3 connection.

3 To create a new connection, double-click the Make New Connection icon.

Make New Connection

4 You will see the first screen of the Make New Connection wizard. Enter a name for the new connection and make sure that your modem is selected. If it isn't, click on the down arrow and select your modem. If it doesn't appear, you haven't installed your modem under Windows. See later in this chapter if you are unsure how to do this. Click Next when you have finished.

Select your installed modem here.

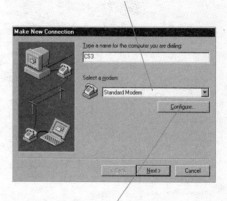

You can check the configuration that is set up with the selected modem via this button.

5 The screen below allows you to enter the telephone number you will be using to connect with the CSi service. Make sure you enter the number exactly as it is shown, including the spaces.

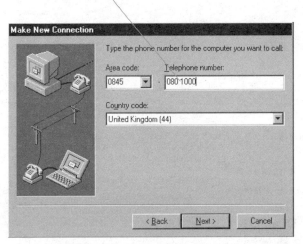

6 This is the last screen of this Wizard. A connection has now been created. Click on Finish and a new CS3 icon will appear in the Dial-Up Networking folder. You can now try and connect to CSi again.

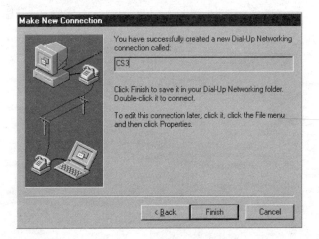

...contd

7 Double-click on the new CS3 Connection and you will see this dialogue box. Enter your password and user ID, then click on the Connect button. Dial-Up Networking will attempt to make a connection to the CSi service.

Some Windows users may notice that their password isn't saved, as they have to enter this each time they log onto CSi. To cure this, when you boot your system, don't click on Cancel when the password dialogue box appears. If you type a password here, you will find that your CSi password will now be saved.

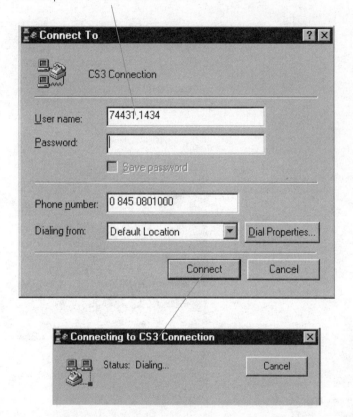

If you have problems dialling CSi from within the CSi software, you can use the CS3 connection utility as a separate program. Double-click on the CS3 icon and connect with the CSi service. Then start the CSi software. You will be able to use the service, as a full connection has been made, even if this wasn't achieved via the CSi software itself.

Installing Your Modem

One of the main problems that is encountered by CSi users when they try and connect to the service is a problem with the modem driver they have installed under Windows. You must have the correct driver set up with your modem if you are to connect successfully. If you look back at step 5 in 'Checking Your CS3 Connection' on page 44, you will see that your installed modem should be visible, or available from the drop-down list. If it is not, follow these steps to install a driver for your modem.

Click on the Start button, then select Settings > Control Panel.

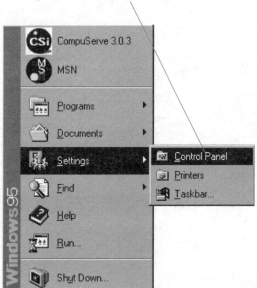

HANDY TIP

Extra information is available on-line on how to install a modem under Windows. Go to the UK Help Forum and look for the file MODINST.DOC.

2 You will see the Control Panel window open. You are looking for the Modems icon. Double-click on this now.

...contd

3 When you click on the Modems icon, this first dialogue box appears. If you have a modem driver installed at all, it will be shown in the main window.

If you have more than one modem available in the window, delete the entries that you don't need.

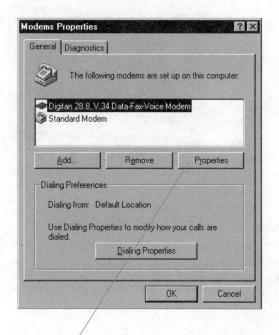

You can check the properties of a driver by highlighting it and then clicking on this button. You will see the dialogue box on the right open. When you are ready, click on the Add button to move to the next screen.

4 This is a Wizard that will take you through the stages of installing a new modem driver.

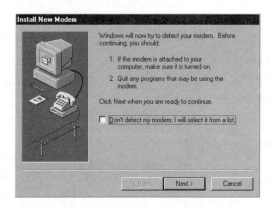

Windows has a database of modems that it knows. If it cannot find yours, it will use the Standard modem. In most cases this will work perfectly well.

If you know which make and model of modem you have, don't tick the box in the centre of the screen; just click Next to choose your modem from a list. If, however, you are not sure of the make and model, let Windows detect it for you.

5 If you have asked Windows to detect your modem, you will see this dialogue box open when you click on Next.

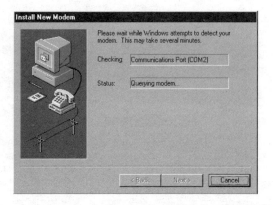

Your modem will be detected and a driver will be entered into the main window as you see in step 3.

...contd

HANDY TIP

If you don't see your make and model, you will need to contact the manufacturer. Ask for the Windows .INF driver for your make and model. Copy this to the C:\WINDOWS\INF folder. You can then go through the auto-detect procedure again.

6 If you didn't ask Windows to auto-detect your modem, another dialogue box will open so that you can select your modem from a list. When you have selected your modem, click on Next to move to the next screen.

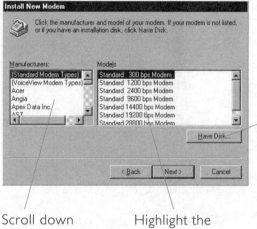

If you have a driver that came with the modem, you can use it by clicking on this button. You will then be able to load the driver from CD-ROM or floppy disk.

Scroll down the list of manufacturers here.

Highlight the make and model of your modem.

7 Windows has now installed your modem driver. Highlight the port that your modem is attached to, then click Next.

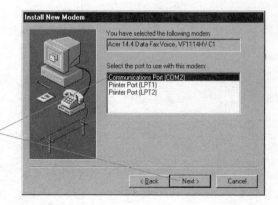

8 This dialogue box confirms that the modem has been set up. Click on the Finish button and you will be taken back to the main modem dialogue as you saw in step 3. You should now see a new entry in the main window.

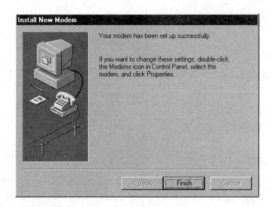

9 Now that you have successfully installed your modem, you can check that it is available by going back to the CS3 Connection dialogue box that you saw in step 5 on page 44. You should now be able to select your modem from the list and use this to connect to CSi.

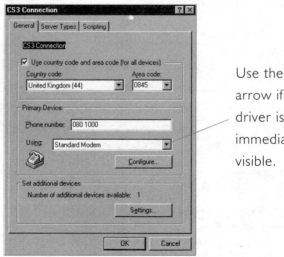

Use the down arrow if the driver isn't immediately visible.

TCP/IP and Dial-Up Adapter

The last components that you must make sure are in place and set up correctly are the TCP/IP protocol and the Dial-Up Adapter. TCP/IP allows your computer to connect to the Internet, as this is a standard set of protocols that have been adopted by the industry as a whole. The other component, the Dial-Up Adapter, works hand-in-hand with TCP/IP, allowing a connection to the server that you are dialling.

You can check if you have these components installed through the Control Panel. If they are missing or you think they may be corrupt, follow these steps to install new components.

1 Open the Control Panel from the Start menu (Settings > Control Panel), then double-click on the Network icon.

Network

2 This dialogue box will open. You should see these components listed in the main window. If not, you will need to install them now. If you think they may be corrupt, highlight each one and click on the Remove button. They will be deleted. You can now follow the rest of the steps in this section to install new components.

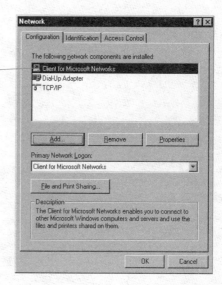

HANDY TIP

If you have other items listed in this window, they shouldn't interfere with CSi. If you do have problems, try removing all of them except the three you see here. Only these items are needed to connect to CSi.

3 Highlight Client for Microsoft Networks and click on the Add button. You will see this dialogue box open. Click on Protocol and then the Add button.

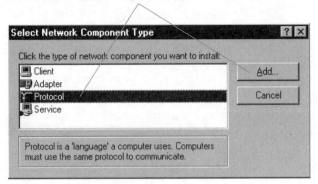

4 Find Microsoft in the list in the window on the left-hand side. When you click on this entry you will see the components available. Click on the TCP/IP entry, then click OK.

You may be asked to insert your Windows CD in order to install the required components.

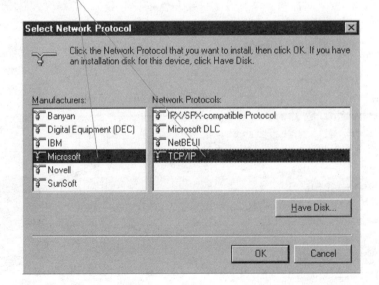

5 You will be returned to the main screen in step 2. This time, highlight Adapter and click on Add.

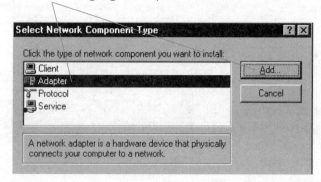

6 This time you will see the Select Network Adapters dialogue box open. Again, select the Microsoft entry from the list in the left-hand window. Click on this when you have found it. You will see the entry on the right change to Dial-Up Adapter. Highlight this and click OK.

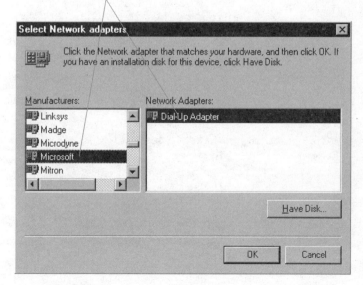

You have now successfully installed the TCP/IP and Dial-Up Adapter components.

Software Fixes

Whenever bugs are identified and solved in the CSi software, CompuServe will release 'fixes' to compensate for them. If you experience any of the problems mentioned below, you will need to get hold of the programs listed.

HANDY TIP If you have not joined any Forums as yet, but would like to fix the bugs that are present in the CSi software, use the search feature of the CSi service. Type in the file name and you will be taken to its location, where you can download it.

No Sound

If you have installed the CSi software but do not have any sound effects, you will need to go to the UK Help Forum and enter the "CS3 for Win95/NT" library. There you will find a file called CS303WAV.EXE. After installing this fix, you will have full sound effects. The lack of sound, however, won't affect the operation of the CSi software.

Customise Toolbar

If you try and customise the toolbar through the Preferences dialogue box with the CSi software, you may find that some or all of the icons in the toolbar set themselves to the 'Heart' icon for favourite places. This won't affect the CSi software, but it does make it difficult to identify each icon's function when they look the same. In the same "CS3" library you will find the file RIBBON.TXT. This will give full instructions about how to resolve this problem.

Country Settings

In some cases, when altering the country setting in the Preferences menu, you may see 'Wales' displayed instead of the country you selected. A fix for this problem is contained in the file COUNTRY.DAT, again in the "CS3" library.

Uninstall

The initial release of the CSi software's uninstall utility didn't operate correctly. CS3OUF.EXE fixes this problem. You can now uninstall the CSi software if you need to.

Getting Started

This chapter covers the main features of the CSi software that you have installed on your computer.

Chapter Three

Covers

The Main Screen

After you have successfully installed the CSi software and configured it, you will be able to take full advantage of the services that CSi provides. If you are back at the Windows desktop, either click on the CSi icon that has been placed on the desktop or choose the CSi entry from the Start menu. The main CSi screen will open.

HANDY TIP

This is a fully functional window and behaves just as any other that you see in Windows. You can minimise or maximise the window whenever you need to.

You access all of the available CSi services from this window. As you saw in the last section, you can also choose whether to have your Internet browser active within the CSi interface, or to open it as an external program.

This is the main icon bar or toolbar:

You will already be familiar with many of the entries in the menu bar, as they follow standard Windows operational practices. Under the Edit menu, for instance, you will find the usual Cut and Paste options.

You can type the address of a Web page you want to view in this box. Your Internet browser will then start and load the Web site.

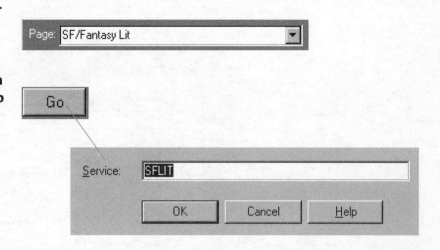

| REMEMBER | **How your Internet browser will be** |

How your Internet browser will be started depends on how you set this up in the Preferences dialogue box. You can have your browser running internally or externally to the CSi software: see page 33 for more information.

The Go button is perhaps – after the e-mail system – the one that most makes the CSi service different from the others. From the Go button you have access to the Forums that make up the vast majority of the CSi service. If you click on this button now, you will see a dialogue box open where you can enter the Forum name.

The rest of the toolbar is filled with icons. These offer quick shortcuts to the main functions of the CSi interface. You don't have to look for the menu entry, just click on the icon. You have full control over how these icons are arranged, as there is a setting dialogue box where you can choose which icons are displayed and which are hidden.

...contd

To customise the icons in the toolbar, do the following:

Select the Preferences entry from the Access drop-down menu, then click on the Toolbar tab.

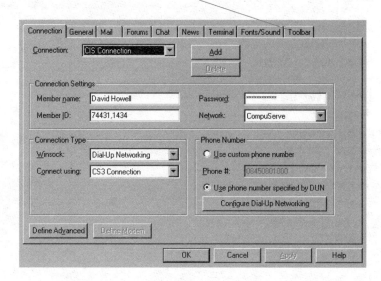

BEWARE

Customising your toolbar is one area in which you may come across one of the CSi bugs. If you experience problems, you will need to get hold of the patch program to fix this. See page 60 for more details.

2 From here you can customise your toolbar with any icon you want. In the list on the left, click on the icon that you want to place in the toolbar. You will see a description of the function of each of the icons as you move down the list.

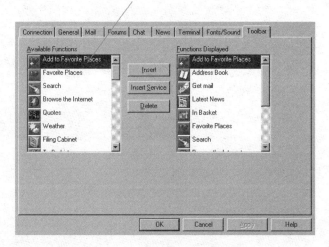

3 When you have selected an icon, click on the 'Insert' button in the middle of the dialogue box. You will see the icon appear as a new entry in the right-hand window.

4 You also have the option of assigning an icon a different function that is not one of the defaults. You do this by highlighting an icon and then clicking on the Insert Service button. You will see this dialogue box pop open.

5 Enter a name and a service in the boxes provided, and then click on a button. When you move back to the main CSi page you will see the new icon in the toolbar.

The icon has now been placed in the toolbar. Just click on it and it will execute whichever function you have assigned to it.

...contd

CSi offers members a quick route to the most widely-used services on the network. Click on any of these large buttons and you will be logged on – if you aren't already – and taken to that part of the service.

HANDY TIP

If you get lost or want to access another part of the service, you can always get back to this screen by clicking on the Main Menu button that is usually displayed on-screen.

Clicking on the Assistance tab reveals these options.

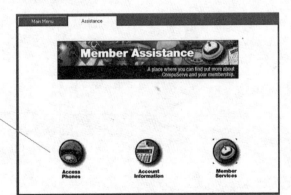

...contd

This is the last section of the CSi main screen.

This clock shows how long you have been on-line.

To reset the clock, click here.

Click here to collect your mail.

You will only see this icon when you are connected to the CSi service.

What's New

What's New

From the Main Menu you can find out what is new on the CSi service by clicking on this button. If you are not connected already, your computer will dial CSi and log you on.

HANDY TIP

If you find that there are a large number of files that you would like to read, save them all now, then read them later, when you have logged off – along with your e-mail. Getting into this habit helps to reduce your phone and CSi service charges.

When the files have loaded, the What's New list will be displayed in a window like the one below.

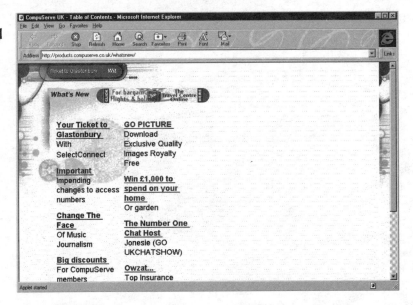

Each link is to a separate file, which you can view, then save if the information is something you find interesting. As you can see, this is an Internet browser (Internet Explorer) that has been set up to open externally to the CSi software when a Web site is accessed. As CSi's service is moving more and more to the Internet, most of the quick access buttons you see on the Main Menu take you to a page on the CompuServe Web site.

Table of Contents

Table of Contents

The next icon along is the Table of Contents. If you click on this you will be taken to another area of the CSi Web site.

REMEMBER

You could just as easily view this screen if you have your Internet browser set to run externally to the CSi software. You can still access this page once you have arrived at the CompuServe home page.

Click the button that interests you. You will then move to that particular page on the CSi Web site.

Internet

Internet

If you want to access the Internet directly, you can start off on the CSi Home page. Clicking on the large Internet icon will take you straight there.

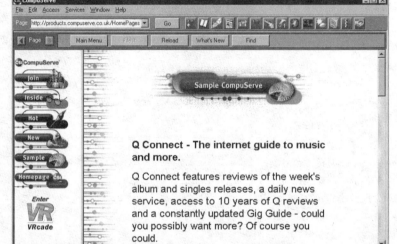

You can still access all of the Web sites by setting-up your Internet browser to run internally within the CSi software. Go to page 33 to do this if you don't want your Web pages to show in an external browser as you see here.

Once there you have total access to the Internet. The CSi Web site provides easy access to some of the popular features, such as search engines and FTP (File Transfer Protocol). As your Web browser is running, you can also enter in any Web address and move directly to that site or page.

Chat

Chat

Chat is one of the main services that CSi provides. You can log on and hold a conversation with anyone else who is on the system. Click on the Chat icon to move to that part of the service.

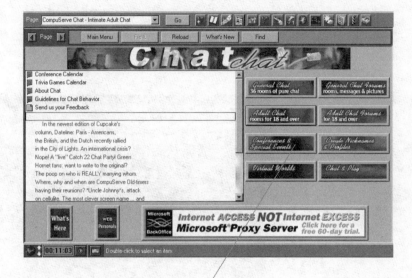

Click on one of these
buttons to move to that
particular Chat area.

Chat is covered in greater detail in Chapter Five.

Forums & Communities

Forums & Communities

Forums are the best-known feature of CSi, and are one of the main reasons that people join the service. At the time of writing there are over 1,600 Forums covering every possible subject. You can post questions, chat to other members and download software. Again, this service is closely linked to the CSi Web site. Clicking on the main icon will take you to that page.

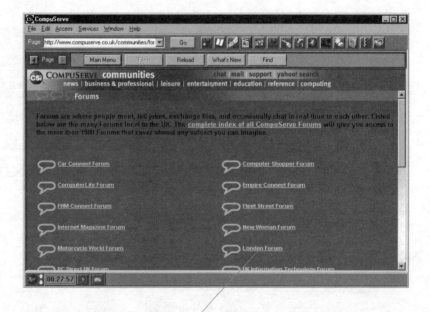

Click on any of the Forums listed. As this is a Web page, most entries on the page that are underlined are links to other pages on the site. Try a few links now.

Access Phone Numbers

Access Phones

If you want to check the access phone numbers that you are using to dial into the CSi network, check if a problem you are encountering has been answered in the Frequently Asked Questions (FAQ), or check the surcharges on an account, you can do all that through this icon.

Any phone numbers that you find you need to change must be entered in the Preferences dialogue box that you saw in the last chapter. Also, make sure that this number is the same one that is set up in Dial-Up Networking and is used with your CS3 connection.

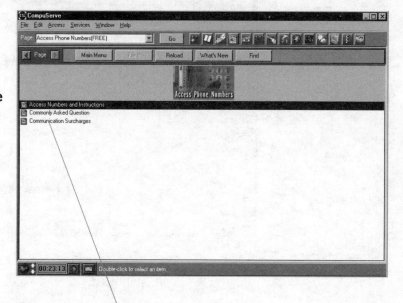

Click on a file that you want to view and it will open in the window.

Account Information

Account Information

This icon gives you access to the information relating to your account. Here you can do everything from changing a password to altering your direct debit instructions.

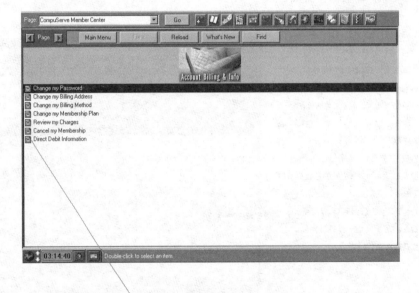

Click on a file that you want to view and it will open in the window.

Member Services

Member Services

When you click on this icon you are taken to a second screen that in turn gives you access to a vast amount of information on the CSi system. On the right of the main screen you can see a number of subject headings. Clicking on one of these takes you to an intermediate screen, which then offers access to the service you want.

HANDY TIP

Use this section of CSi along with on-line help, which you can always access through the Help drop-down menu on the main CSi screen.

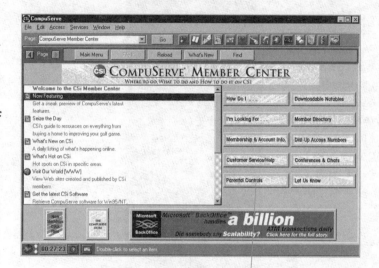

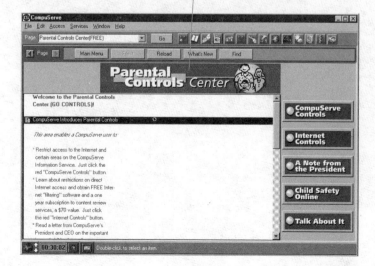

Home Desktop

The last section of the main screen allows access to the vast majority of CSi's services.

 You always have quick access to these buttons by clicking on the Main Menu button that you will see on-screen as you move around the CSi service, as you can see on the opposite page.

The vast majority of the services under these headings can be accessed and set up before you log on. You can set up a search or write some e-mail, then connect and carry out all the tasks you need to. This saves you money, as you will then be connected for the least amount of time. The last two areas, My Information and Learn About, allow you to store private information for later use and also offer easy access to on-line help and tutorials on all of CSi's services.

Main Menu

This button always returns you to the main CSi window. You will see a similar button in a lot of services. In both cases, if you find yourself confused about where you are in the CSi service you can always get back to the main menu by clicking on this button.

In this example the Main Menu button appears in the toolbar of the Access Phone Numbers dialogue box. Click on this to go straight back to the familiar main menu.

Go

Through the Go button you have a quick and easy route to the Forums and Communities that make CSi so attractive to members. The Go screen offers a more comprehensive interface to this section of the service. You can jump straight to your favourite Forums that you saved in a previous session on-line, do some housekeeping by deleting Forums you no longer visit, or take a look in the Directory for new Forums to visit.

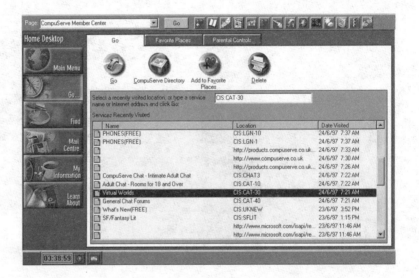

| Select a Forum.

2 Click on the Go button to move to that Forum.

Find

CSi is so vast that trying to find something on the service can often be a daunting task. The Find button allows you to search for files, members on the systems and even references to topics on the Internet.

HANDY TIP

If you use the Search Internet button, you will also have access to other search engines on the Internet, such as Yahoo! and Alta Vista, which may be of use if you can't find what you are looking for straight away.

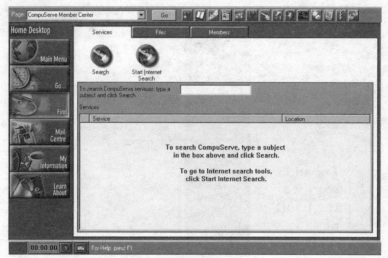

I Select the Service, Files or Members tabs.

2 Click on the Search button.

Mail Centre

E-mail is amongst the most essential services for a vast majority of users. The CSi software allows you to have full control over the messages that you receive and those that you send to other CSi members or anyone in the world with an e-mail address.

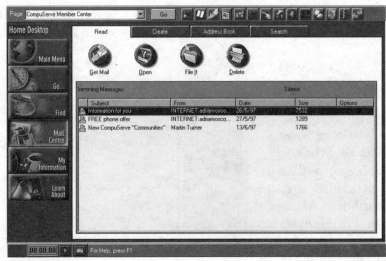

HANDY TIP

Try and get into the habit of composing all of your outgoing mail before you log on. This will save you a great deal of time and help to keep your on-line charges to the minimum.

Mail is covered in greater depth in Chapter Four.

My Information

There will always be some information that you will want to be able to view even when you are not connected to the CSi service. You can file this information away in the My Information section of the CSi software. You can create a things-to-do list, prioritise them and perform searches.

HANDY TIP **Some screens of the CSi service feature a File It button which allows you to save the contents of the screen. The My Information area is provided for this purpose.**

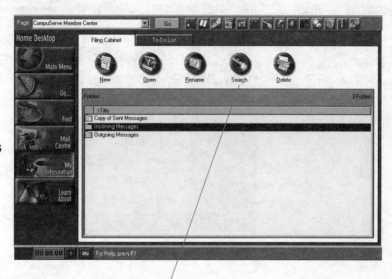

The Search button allows you to search all of your saved files for items matching any criteria you specify.

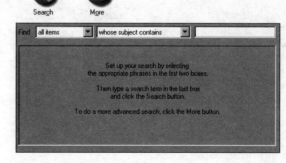

Learn About

CSi can be a confusing place, especially for new users. As with most modern software, CSi has on-line help to give you all the information you need to make the most from the service.

You also have access to on-line help through the Help drop-down menu.

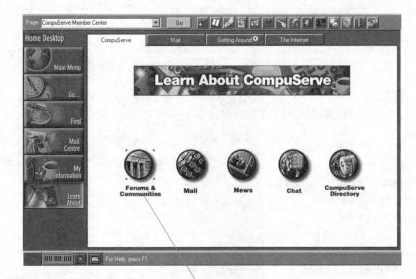

Clicking on any of these buttons links to a screen that provides information on the requested topic.

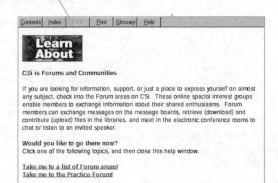

Mail

Millions of e-mail messages are sent each day from every corner of the world. CSi automatically gives you an e-mail account which you can use to send and receive messages. In this chapter you will learn how to make the most from this part of your membership.

Chapter Four

Covers

The Mail Centre

You can always get back to this icon by clicking on the Main Menu button that appears on most of CompuServe's pages.

All of your e-mail functions are grouped together in one area of the CSi service. Click on the Mail Centre button from the Main Menu now.

The main Mail Centre screen will open, as you see below.

Click here to retrieve your mail.

Use this icon to open a message. You can also double-click on the message in the main window.

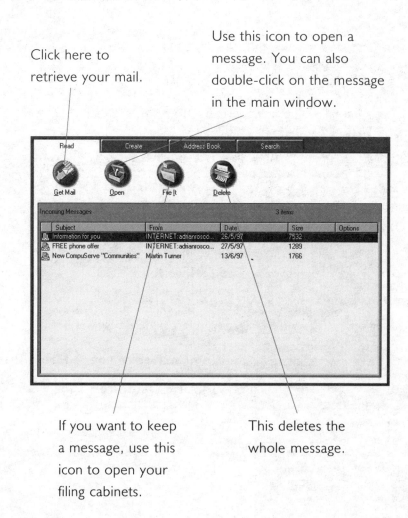

If you want to keep a message, use this icon to open your filing cabinets.

This deletes the whole message.

The Get Mail Icon

When you have connected to the CSi service you can pick up your mail. If you have any mail, a message at the bottom of the Main Menu screen next to the envelope icon will inform you of this. To pick up your mail do the following:

1 Click on the Mail Centre icon.

2 You will now see the Mail Centre's main screen. Click on the Get Mail icon.

When you first start the CSi software, you can click on the envelope icon to retrieve your mail. This has the same effect as using the Get Mail icon in the Mail Centre.

3 Your mail will be retrieved and put in your mail box for you to read now or later.

The Open Icon

When your mail has been retrieved, you can read it by highlighting a message and clicking on the Open icon on the toolbar.

1 Highlight the message.

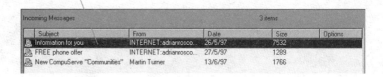

2 Click on the Open icon.

3 Your message opens in the reader.

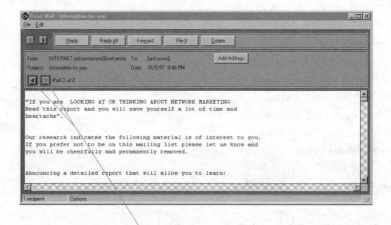

Use these buttons to move forwards and backwards through the messages.

The File It Icon

If the message that you have been sent has something that you need to keep, you can do this with the next icon on the toolbar. The File It icon does just what it says: it allows you to file the contents of a message for future reference.

REMEMBER

If you are looking at pages of information on the Internet, the File It icon may not be available. You can still save Internet pages by using the browser's own Save feature. To do this, however, you will need to use the browser externally to the CSi software.

1 Click on the File It icon now.

File It

2 This dialog box will open. Choose an existing folder to save your message to.

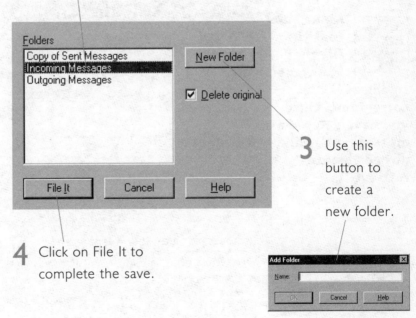

Folders

Copy of Sent Messages
Incoming Messages
Outgoing Messages

New Folder

☑ Delete original

File It   Cancel   Help

3 Use this button to create a new folder.

4 Click on File It to complete the save.

Add Folder   ☒

Name:

OK   Cancel   Help

The Delete Icon

The last of the main icons on the Mail Centre toolbar is the standard Delete icon. If you have read your message and you don't want to keep it, you can use this icon to delete the message.

Click on the Delete icon.

Delete

You will see this warning message pop-up each time you do this unless you disable this dialogue box by removing the tick in the box.

Make sure that the file that you want to delete is the correct one. Once you have deleted a message, you will not be able to retrieve it.

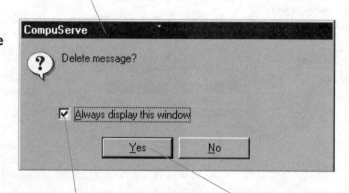

2 Removing the tick from this box will mean that you will not be given this warning when deleting subsequent messages.

3 Click here to delete the message.

Reading Mail

Now that we have covered the main icons that you will see on the Mail Centre's toolbar, we will now look at how you read and reply to your mail messages. Open a message by either double-clicking on it in the main window, or by highlighting it and then clicking on the Open icon. You will see a window like the one below open with your message.

REMEMBER

You don't need to be connected to CSi when you read your mail. You can collect your messages and then read them when you log off the service.

Use these buttons to move through all the messages that are in your mail box. You don't have to keep closing this window and choosing another message. These buttons will do this for you. Notice that the sender of the mail changes to keep you informed about whose message you are reading.

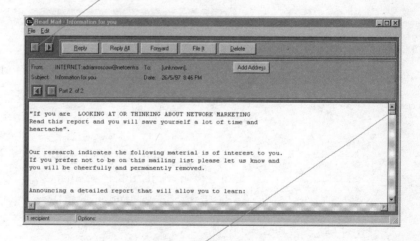

Use the scroll bars as you would a normal window to move through the message as you read it. Alternatively, use the up and down arrow keys on your keyboard.

Replying to Mail

After you have read your mail you will often want to send responses. Click on the Reply button and this window will open:

REMEMBER

You don't have to send each message one at a time. CSi allows you to build up an out-basket of messages that will be sent when you next log onto CSi.

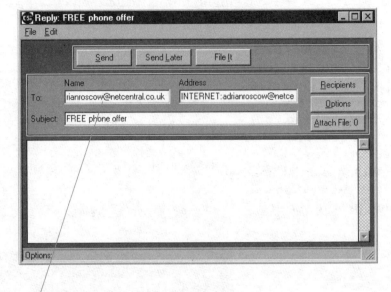

2 From this window you can simply send a message back to the sender's address: the address is entered automatically for you.

3 When you have completed your message, click on Send to have it sent immediately, or click on the adjacent icon to have it sent later. It will be stored with your other outgoing messages and entered as a to-do task for the next time you log onto CSi.

4 File It opens the dialogue box that you saw on page 81. You can use it to store your messages for future reference.

...contd

In the Reply window that you saw on the last page, you will notice three extra buttons on the right-hand side of the window. These offer you extra functions to enhance your messages.

Message Recipients
This dialogue box allows you to build a list of every person you would like to receive a copy of your message.

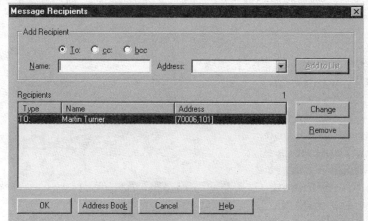

HANDY TIP

If you type a partial name into the name box, and if that name is in your address book, the rest of the name will be entered for you automatically.

To:
This name is the primary recipient of the message.

cc:
These people get a carbon copy of the message being sent.

bcc:
These people get a blind carbon copy of the message. (Only the sender and receiver will know about it.)

...contd

The functions of the buttons in the Message Recipients dialogue box are explained below.

Add to List

Adds the information in the Name and Address boxes. Highlight the name in the main list and then click on the Add to List button.

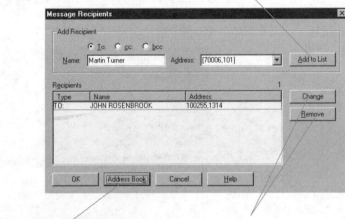

Your numerical CSi email address is only used when you log on. You can use the person's proper name (or nickname if they use one) when sending mail. You will also see in Forums and when you do searches that a member's name is always shown with their user ID.

Change

Allows you to change a highlighted entry in the Recipients list.

Remove

Allows you to delete a highlighted entry.

Address Book

Allows you to automatically add to the Recipients list addresses that you have stored previously.

You have full control over who will receive a copy of your replies to any messages that you get.

...contd

Searching for someone's CSi e-mail address

If you don't have the address of a person you want to send e-mail to, you can use a function of your address book to search for them on the CSi system.

| As you did on the last page, click on the Message Recipients button. You will see the address book open.

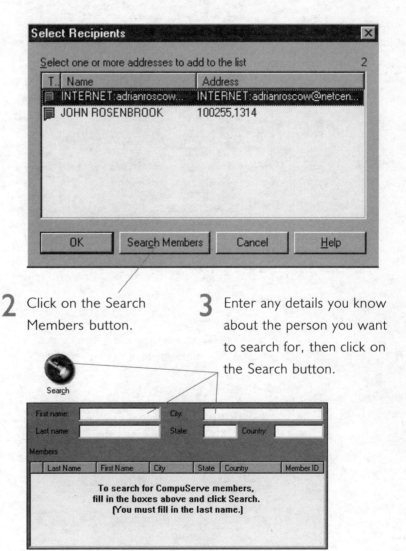

2 Click on the Search Members button.

3 Enter any details you know about the person you want to search for, then click on the Search button.

Options

Below the Recipients button in the Reply window is the Options button. This allows you to set certain parameters for each message that you send.

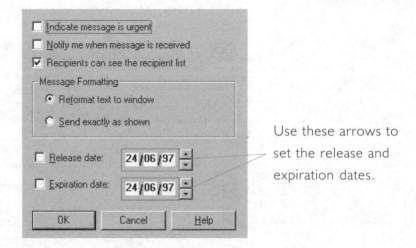

Use these arrows to set the release and expiration dates.

Indicate message is urgent
Ticking this box gives the message the highest priority. When your recipient receives the message they will see this status before they open the message.

Notify me when message is received
When your recipient opens the message, a copy will be sent to you.

Recipients can see the recipient list
Indicates if the recipients will be able to see the names of all of the other people who received this message.

Reformat text to window
Makes sure that the message will fit into the recipient's window, wrapping the text as needed.

...contd

Send exactly as shown
Makes sure that any paragraph spacing or formatting is not changed when the message is sent.

Release date
The message will only be sent on the date you input here.

Expiration date
The message will be deleted from the recipient's mailbox on this date if they haven't already downloaded it.

Just about anything digital can be attached to an e-mail message. Think carefully, however, before you attach a large file to a message. The recipient may not appreciate having to wait for the whole e-mail plus its attachments to download when they logon. This will increase their logon time, which can get very expensive.

Attach File
As well as the text that you write to form your message, you also have the option of sending attached files along with it to your recipient. These can be other text files or even images.

To attach a file, follow these steps:

After you have finished writing your message, click on the Attach File button.

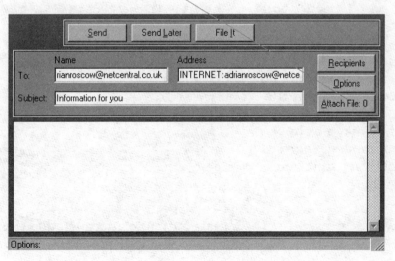

...contd

You can have more than one file attached to your e-mail if you wish. But again, take into account the time it will take for you to transmit the whole message, and for the recipient to download it when it arrives.

2 You will see the familiar Windows file-selection dialogue box open. Select a file you want to attach to your e-mail message, then click on the Open button.

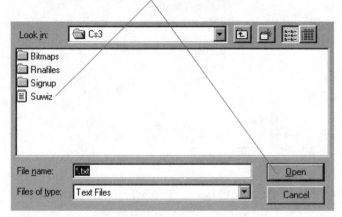

3 This dialogue box will appear, displaying the name of the file you have just chosen. Select the file type from the drop-down list.

Think before you send graphic files. Will the person to whom you are sending this file be able to view it? They may not have the same graphics software that you have.

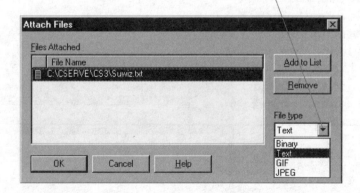

Add To List
Use this button to attach another file. You will be taken back to the Windows file-selection dialogue box, as in step 2.

Remove
This button deletes the file in the main window.

4 If you now click OK in the Attach File dialogue box, the file you have chosen will be attached to the e-mail message. Notice that the Attach File button on the main mail screen has now changed: it shows the number of attachments that will be sent with the message.

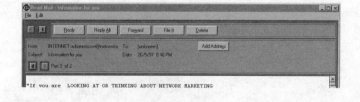

Adding Entries to the Address Book

You may have noticed in the Read Mail screen (page 86) that there was a button labelled 'Add Address'. This allows you to add to your address book the e-mail address of someone who has sent you mail.

| Click the Add Address button.

You can modify the information contained on each person as and when you need to. Treat this just as you would a paper-based address book.

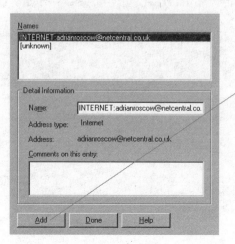

2 Click the Add button to confirm that you want to add this address to your address book.

Navigating Using the Tabs

The Create, Address Book and Search tabs are a quick route to these functions of the Mail Centre. All of the features are accessible through the mail-reading main screen, as you have seen on the previous pages. However, if you want to check an address book entry, search for a member, or create a new e-mail message from scratch (i.e., one that isn't a reply to one you have received), you can carry out all these tasks by clicking on the appropriate tab.

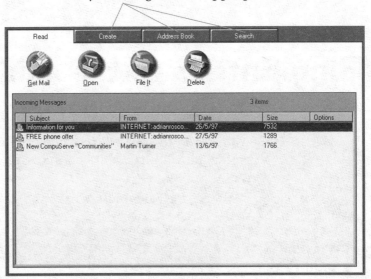

You will always see this screen when you click on the Mail Centre button from the Main Menu screen.

Chat

Chapter Five

The Chat areas of the CSi service are just that – places where people can come together to chat about every kind of subject. In this chapter you will see how you can join one of the many chat areas and talk with a group or have a private conversation with another CSi member.

Covers

The Main Menu

Chat

From the main CSi screen, click on the Chat icon. If you are not already connected to CSi, your computer will dial out and connect you to the service. Once there, you will see the main Chat window open.

BEWARE

Virtual Worlds is a virtual reality area. You will need to download the special software and install this on your computer before you will be able to participate in this area.

This main screen allows you to move around the Chat area. To begin with, click on the What's Here button on the bottom left of your screen.

What's New

In the main window you will see a number of files and an explanation of what each one contains. You can use these to find useful information and announcements about this part of the service. When you have finished, move back to the main Chat screen by clicking on the back arrow at the top of the screen.

 HANDY TIP

Notice that you can enter the search area of CSi from this screen. This allows you to search for a member or any information on the CSi service.

You can click here to move back to the main screen.

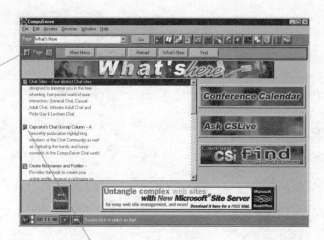

If there is a file that you want to look at, double-click on it. It will open in the main window, as you see below.

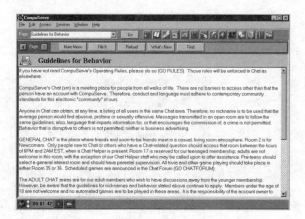

2 If the file is something you may want to refer to in the future, you can save it. Click on the File It button at the top of the screen.

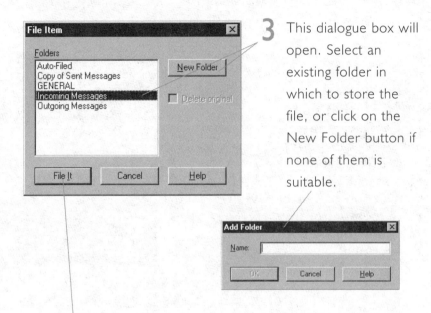

3 This dialogue box will open. Select an existing folder in which to store the file, or click on the New Folder button if none of them is suitable.

4 Click on the File It button to save the file in the selected folder. You will then see the dialogue box below appear to confirm this. Click OK to complete to task.

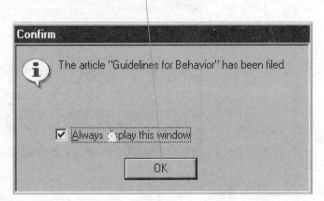

Welcome

This is the main welcome screen for Chat. You may find this familiar, as many of the welcome screens for the CSi service look similar to this one.

HANDY TIP

Try and get into the habit of checking this section of the service regularly. You can then keep up-to-date with what's happening on the CSi service.

As with other areas of the CSi service, you can click the Read Announcements icon to catch up with the latest news. The latest announcements are displayed in their own window, shown below.

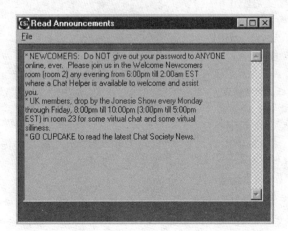

Chat

This is the main Chat window. From here you can navigate around the Chat area of your choice and hold conversations with anyone who is also in the Chat area; you can even hold a private conversation with another member. Before moving on to participate in a Chat session, you can check a few things from this main screen.

Click on the Chat button to enter the Chat area.

As with all of CSi's main screens, you can click on the Learn About button for detailed information about the area of the service you are in.

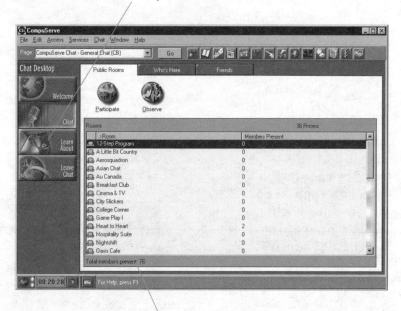

This shows the total number of members currently logged on. You will see this change in real time as members enter and leave the Chat area.

REMEMBER

You can access the other areas of the CSi service from Chat if you need to. You can enter Internet addresses and access Web sites, write e-mail, or move back to the Main Menu and go to a Forum. You are not isolated from the rest of the CSi service when you enter the Chat area.

2 Click on the Who's Here tab.

To start a private chat with someone else in the Chat area, choose their name from the list in the large window, then click on this icon.

If you would like to participate in a group chat, use this icon.

Each member has a profile. You can view anyone's with this icon.

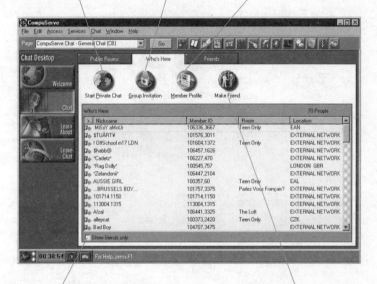

Click here if you want to see only those members in the Chat area who are on your Friends list.

This icon allows you to put a member's details in a special Friends area. Just as with an address book, you can look up a name whenever you like.

3 Click on the Friends tab.

Use this icon to add a new member to your Friends list.

Use this icon to delete an entry.

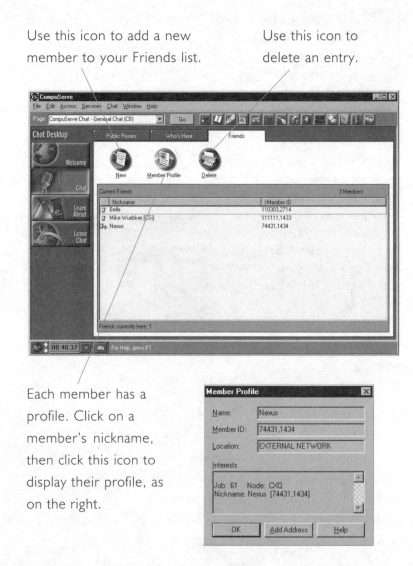

Each member has a profile. Click on a member's nickname, then click this icon to display their profile, as on the right.

This completes our tour through the screens that you can access from the main window when you enter the Chat area. We will now move on to look at Chat in more detail, examining how you can join a group chat and have a private conversation with a CSi member.

Observe

Observe

The other main icon on the opening screen of a Chat area is Observe. As its name suggests, you can go to a Chat area and observe what is being said before you decide if you would like to join in or not. This is like listening to a conversation at a party before you move closer and contribute yourself.

Use this button to find out who's in this Chat room. You may find that there is someone you know already here.

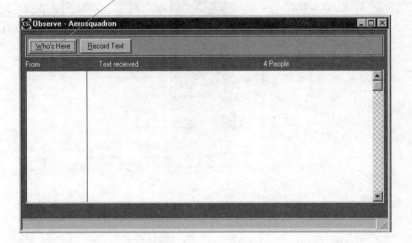

Notice that in this screen you do not have an area where you can type responses. You can see how many people are in this room, who they are and what they are saying to each other. If you want more detailed information about a participant, you can get this by using the Who's Here button. You can then see who the nickname belongs to and any other information that is available about that member.

Participate

Participate is where you enter the Chat area proper. This is a live Chat area where you can talk to anyone in the room in real time.

1 Choose a Chat room to enter by highlighting it with your mouse.

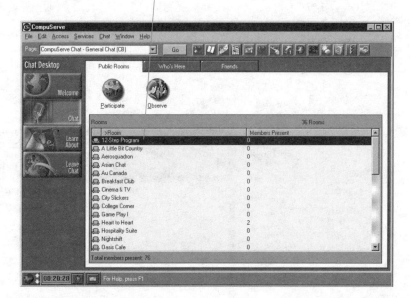

You can only participate in one Chat area at a time.

2 Click on the Participate icon.

Participate

...contd

Remember this is a general Chat area. It is like having a group discussion. If you see something that you would like to have a chat about specifically, request a private chat with that person. You can see how to do this in step 5 on page 110.

3 This is the main Chat screen. Here you can see what is being said in the room and write your own contributions to the conversations that are going on.

The name that appears here is the user who is typing the text opposite.

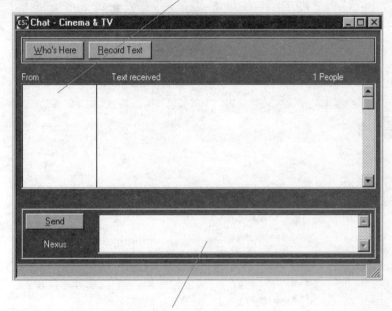

You can record the convers- ation you are having by clicking on the Record button at any time. Notice that it will change to Stop Recording when you do this.

Type your responses to the text you see in the main screen here. Click on the send button or hit the Return key on your keyboard when you have finished.

4 Clicking on the Who's Here button will bring up this dialogue box, allowing you to see who is in the Chat room at this time.

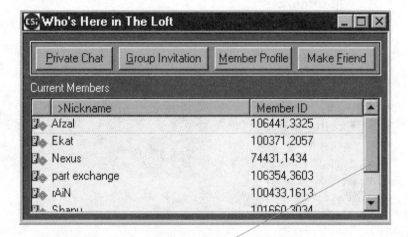

Use the scroll bar to move down the list.

5 If you would like to have a private chat with any of the people in the room, highlight their name in the list in step 4 and then click on the Private Chat button. This window will open.

REMEMBER

This is a private Chat area. Unless you consent for someone else to join you in this conversation, no one else can see your conversation on-screen.

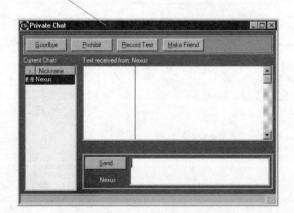

...contd

Along the top of the Private Chat dialogue box you will see four buttons. These help you manage your chat sessions.

Goodbye

Click on this button to exit from a private chat with a member.

Prohibit

Here, you can select people who are not allowed to participate in a chat with you by adding them to a Prohibited list.

Use the Prohibit button to regulate who you talk to in Chat. Don't be afraid to put someone on your Prohibited list. You can remove them from it at any time. This way you always have control over who you talk to in this area of the CSi service.

Use this option to add someone to the Prohibited list permanently. They will be excluded until you take them off the list.

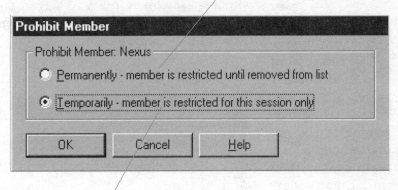

With this option, the member is still added to the Prohibited list, but this exclusion is restricted to the current session.

Record Text

Click on this button to record the text of the current conversation. This button has exactly the same function as the Record Text button in the main Chat window – see page 109.

Make Friend

If you want to add a member to your personal address book, you can do so with this button. You will see the dialogue box below open. You should then confirm that you do want to add them to your address book.

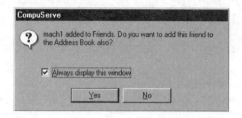

The Group Invitation button

There is one last button that we haven't looked at yet, which we saw in step 4 on page 110. The Group Invitation button opens a similar window to General and Private Chat, as you can see below.

Make sure you know what kind of Chat area you are in before you begin a conversation. If you want to have a private chat with a member, you must be in Private Chat mode, or any other member will be able to see your conversation.

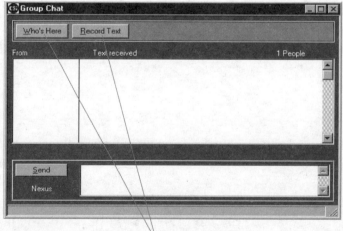

Use these buttons to check who is in this area of Chat, and to record the conversation if you want to. This is just like the main Chat window that you opened in step 4, but here you only talk privately to one person.

Forums

This chapter will show you how to use the many Forums that CSi has on offer.

Chapter Six

Covers

Forums

Forums & Communities

Forums are specialised areas of the CSi service, a bit like the Chat area that you have already seen. Here you can get information, have a chat with someone with the same interest as you, or catch up on the latest information on that particular topic. CSi currently has over 1,600 Forums for you to choose from.

When you first log onto the CSi service you will see the familiar opening screen with its icons. To access the Forums area of the service, click on the Forums & Communities icon at the far right of the screen.

You will see the screen below. You now have access to the whole Forum area, as well as the new Communities service, which will be looked at in more detail in the following chapter.

Many of the Forums that you can join also have a Go command. Use this as a quick way of moving to the Forum that interests you.

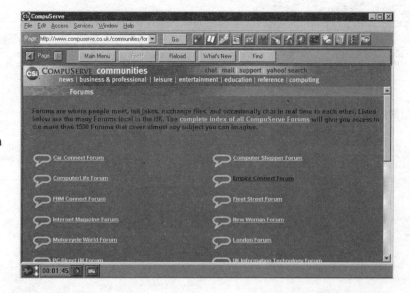

The Forums that you can see listed in the main body of the window on the previous page are hosted by well-known organisations. You can move to any of these Forums by clicking on any of the names. Any text that is underlined is a hyperlink to another part of the CSi service. This works in exactly the same way as if you had accessed a Web site on the Internet. The Forums and Communities areas of the CSi service are Web-based, and behave as Web pages, even though they are linked to the other areas of the CSi service that aren't Web-based.

If you are new to the Forums, or you just want to see what is available from the many Forums that are active at the moment, you can search the database of Forums for those that might interest you.

1 On the opening screen you will see a hyperlink that will take you to the search area of the Forums service. Click on this now.

Forums are where people meet, tell jokes, exchange files, and occasionally chat in real time to each other. Listed below are the many Forums local to the UK. The complete index of all CompuServe Forums will give you access to the more than 1500 Forums that cover almost any subject you can imagine.

2 This is the main search screen. You can scroll manually down the list with the scroll bars.

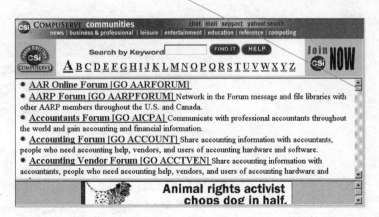

...contd

HANDY TIP

The search engine is best used to search for keywords. These can appear anywhere in the Forum title or description. You will often see Forums shown that you were not previously aware of, particularly if the subject isn't the first word in the subject title – as in the Archive Films Forum. If you had clicked on 'F' for film, you may not have seen this Forum listed.

3 The search engine is very easy to use. Enter a subject name in the box provided and click on the 'Find It' button. You will be taken to any Forums that are available that have that subject. If you need any help with this, click the 'Help' button. This will explain how the search engine works in detail.

As you saw on the opening screen, each Forum title is underlined, indicating that you can link to the Forum by clicking on its name.

4 Click on the name of a Forum that interests you, and you will be taken to it.

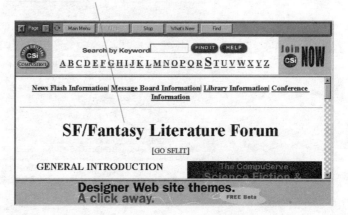

...contd

5 At the top of this page you will see more text that is underlined. This opens other pages that will give you further information before you enter the Forum proper. Click on any of these links to read the text.

You can see a 'Go' command on each of the Forum pages. This just indicates the Go command to enter this Forum from the main screen when you log on. Clicking on this link will only take you to the information page of the CompuServe Web site.

6 To enter the Forum proper, click on the graphic on the first page. You can always tell if a graphic is a link to another screen by moving your mouse pointer over it. If the pointer changes to a pointing hand as you see below, it is a linked graphic. Click on the graphic when you are ready to enter the Forum you have chosen.

CompuServe hosts a number of Forums that are linked to well-known organisations. You can chat to other readers of a magazine, or read information about an organisation you are a member of, or would like to join. When you first enter the Forums and Communities area after you have logged on, you can see these listed in the main window. You first saw this screen on page 114. These Forums behave slightly differently than the others on the service.

1 Choose a Forum that you would like to enter from the list. As this is a hyperlinked piece of text, you can simply click on it. Note that your mouse pointer changes shape, as it did when you entered the Forum in the last topic. In this case we are going to enter the Forum for Car Connect.

2 If you have not been to this Forum before, you will be presented with this dialogue box. Enter your name and list any relevant interests, then click on the 'Join' button.

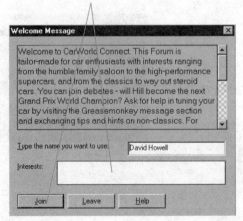

3 Another dialogue box will now open that will allow you to view files that you might find of interest. This is the announcement screen.

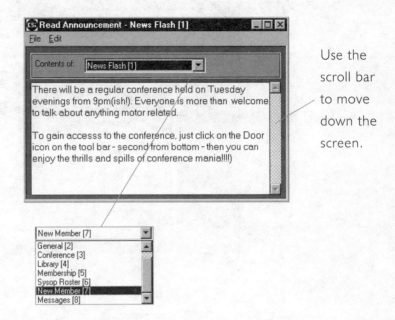

Use the scroll bar to move down the screen.

When you have finished reading the announcements, close the window to move to the main screen.

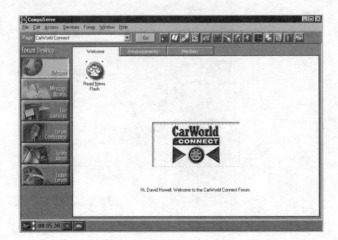

Message Board

On the main screen, you have the usual buttons on the left-hand side of the window. Click on the Message Board button now to move to the next screen.

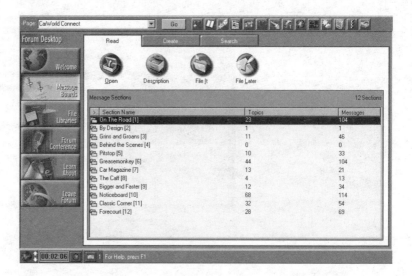

To read a text file, highlight it, then either click on the Open icon, or click on Description to see a full explanation of what the file contains.

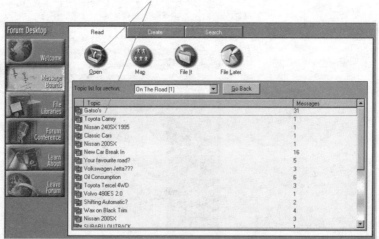

...contd

2 Once you have clicked on the Open icon, the file is displayed in its own window, as in the main screen below.

3 Click here if you want to save the message for later reference.

This screen behaves in a very similar way to the one you use to send and read mail messages. Remember that this is an open Forum. Consider what you say before replying to an existing message, or contributing to the Forum as a whole.

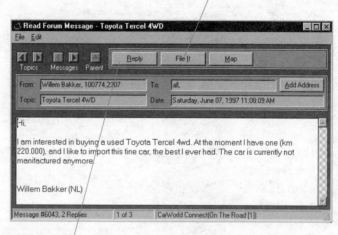

4 Click here to reply to the message. The following window is opened to allow you to compose your new message.

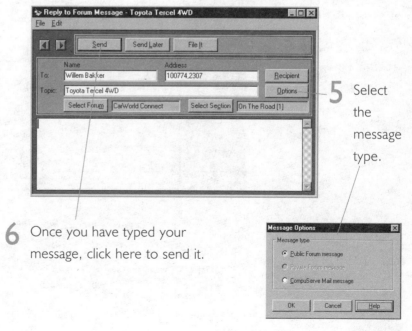

5 Select the message type.

6 Once you have typed your message, click here to send it.

File Libraries

You can view any of the files in the library section of the Forum in much the same way as you looked at the messages posted on the Message Board in the last topic. Highlight a file you are interested in, then click on the Open icon.

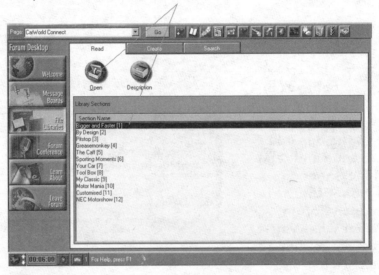

REMEMBER

If you know that there is a file that you would like to see, but cannot seem to locate it, don't forget that this screen has a search engine for you to use. Click on the Search tab to access it.

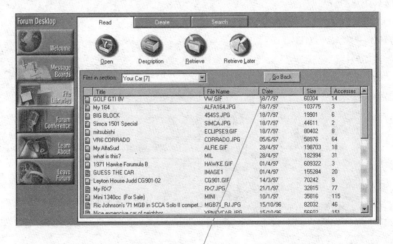

The Go Back button allows you to move to the previous screen you visited. You don't have to start from the main Forum screen each time you want to access a new area of the Forum.

Communities

This chapter will show you how to use the new CompuServe Communities areas.

Chapter Seven

Overview

CompuServe has gone back to the drawing board and redesigned the main area of information that members can access as part of their membership. This information has now been organised into Communities, which are grouped into seven categories. This chapter will look closely at each category and at how you can make the most of the new-look service.

HANDY TIP

CSi is moving more of its services to the Internet. If you are accessing pages from within your CSi software, it is a good idea before looking at any of the new Communities to reset your Internet browser to run externally, in order to take full advantage of the Communities Web pages. You saw how to do this on page 33 in Chapter Two.

There are a number of ways in which you can access the new Communities.

After you have logged onto the CSi service you will see the usual main screen. You can use the Go command to access a new page, Contents, on the CompuServe Web site, which will give you full details.

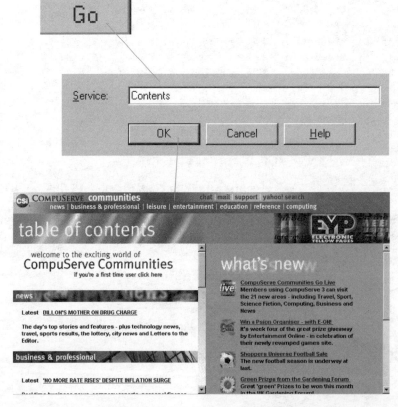

...contd

2 You can also access the Contents page by using the Contents icon that is always displayed when you first log on to the CSi service.

Table of Contents

3 The final way you can access the new Communities service is with the main Forums & Communities icon. This will take you to the main Forums screen that you saw on page 114. From here you can access all of CSi's Forums as well as all of the new Communities.

Forums & Communities

REMEMBER

You always have full access to the Mail and Chat areas of the CSi service when you are using any of the new Communities. Click on the buttons to move straight to these services when you want to.

When you have moved to the new Communities section of CSi, you will always see this status bar displayed, no matter which community you are accessing at the time. You can then easily jump between Communities without having to go back to the main screen each time.

You can access the UK version of Yahoo!, the famous Internet search engine, with this button.

...contd

CSi's new Communities use the familiar Internet interface to allow you to move around the pages and access the services on offer.

When you access a Community you don't have to wait until the whole page has loaded before you can follow any of its hyperlinks: you can click on a hyperlink as soon as you see it.

Most of the new Communities' pages are made up of hyperlinks. These are special elements on the page that you can click on in order to move to another page in the Community. A hyperlink can be a word or a graphic anywhere on the page. You can easily spot which elements are hyperlinks by using your mouse. As you move it across the screen, you will see it change from the normal pointer to a pointing hand. This indicates that the area of the screen that your pointer is over is a hyperlink. Clicking on it will take you to another page in the same Community.

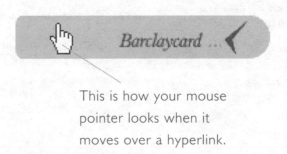

This is how your mouse pointer looks when it moves over a hyperlink.

These are some of the main graphic elements that are hyperlinks on the opening page when you enter the Communities area.

- national & international
- weather

- sport
- business
- technology
- entertainment
- royal

- travel

All Communities carry these types of entries on each page. You use these to move to other areas of the Community that you find interesting.

On some Community pages you will only have this small arrow symbol to click on. It may indicate that you can move forward to another page, or backwards to a page you have already visited.

Weekday Bulletin

If you have problems hearing the bulletin, try <u>downloading</u> the latest Real Audio player.

Hyperlinks on Web pages usually appear like this. Any text that you see underlined is usually a link to another page in the Community.

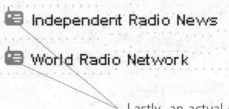

Independent Radio News

World Radio Network

Lastly, an actual graphic may be the hotspot, as in this case.

News

The new-look News Community looks like an electronic newspaper. You can read the latest news headlines and other stories that are making the news. The service is updated each day, so you can stay up-to-date with what is happening in the world.

As well as the top stories, you can read more specialised news by clicking on these entries. Each one is a link to further news pages.

You still have full access to the Mail and Chat areas of CSi when you are in any of the new Communities, as these buttons are always displayed.

REMEMBER

The main news stories have an arrow graphic next to them. Click on the arrow to read a more in-depth report on that particular story.

Use the scroll bars to view the rest of the screen.

As you can see, you have full access to the news services that are available on CSi, from lottery results to CNN. As an example, click on the CNN button at the bottom of the screen now. You will be taken to the now familiar Forum screens. This is how you access these areas of the new Communities. You will see the dialogue box on the opposite page open to give you the latest announcements.

...contd

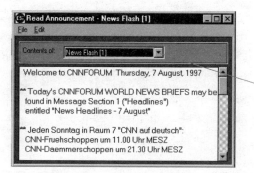

Use the Contents drop-down menu to read more news and announcements from CNN as you did in the CarWorld Forum on page 119.

As you can see, accessing the CNN service is through the usual Forum screen. In this case you can see the files available on the Message Board. Use this screen as you would any of the other Forum screens.

HANDY TIP

You can go back to the Forums and Communities page at any time by using the Leave Forum button. You can then choose another Community to visit.

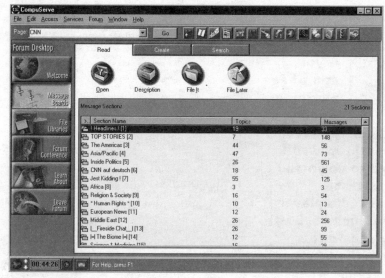

As well as reading the news, you can also listen to the news through the radio button on the News page. Click on the Radio button at the bottom of the page to move to this section of the News Community.

Radio News

Click here to listen to the latest radio news bulletin.

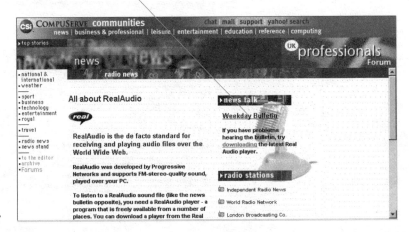

HANDY TIP

If you don't hear anything when you click on the Weekly Bulletin, you will need to download the latest RealAudio player from their Web site. Try and do this when the Internet is quiet (i.e., when most of America is asleep), and phone charges are low. Very early Sunday morning is a very good time!

This is the RealAudio player. If you don't see this open when you try and listen to a radio bulletin, you don't have the latest version of the software. Download it now.

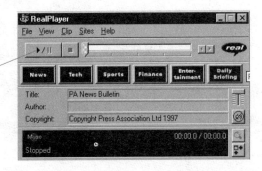

Business & Professional

The business user is well catered for in the new CSi Communities. If you use the service as part of your business, perhaps for e-mail and Internet usage, you will find a great deal of information in this community. Click on the Business & Professional button now to move to this Community's first screen.

Catch up on what made the news on each day of the current week.

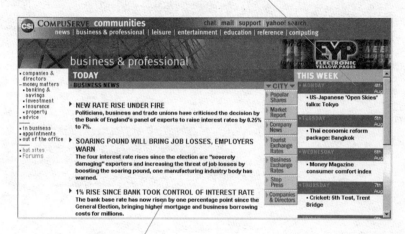

The latest news from the business world is displayed here, and is updated daily. Click on the arrow to see the complete report.

As you can see, there is a great deal of information here to take in. Apart from the news that is presented here on the opening page, there are a large number of buttons that take you to other parts of this Community. As with all the other Communities, if you move the mouse pointer over the screen, you know you have moved over a hyperlink when it changes to the pointing hand. Clicking here will take you to the next screen in the chain.

As an example of the kind of information that anyone in business might need, we are going to take a look at the Business Exchange Rates screen.

1 If you have moved from the first screen in the Business & Professional Community, move back there now.

2 Click on the Business Exchange Rates button.

3 This screen will open.

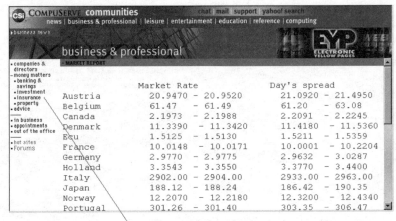

REMEMBER **You can always move back to the start screen by clicking on the Business News button. As you can see, it has an arrow near it. This is a hyperlink to the last screen. You can tell that this is a link, as the mouse pointer turns into a pointing hand when it passes over it.**

These hyperlinks are visible no matter which screen you are on. You therefore have full access from whichever screen you are on in the Community.

The entries on the left of the screen are also links to other parts of this Community. One example is the Banking & Savings entry. If you click on this you will see the following screen.

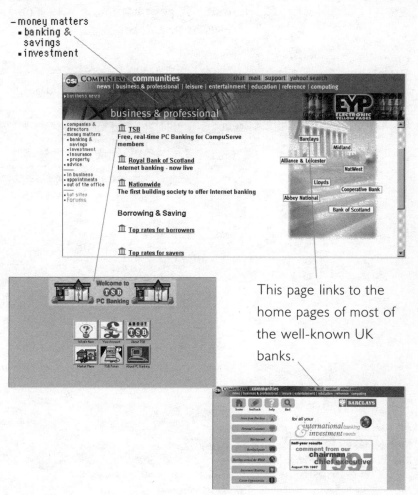

This page links to the home pages of most of the well-known UK banks.

In the past, CSi members who were also TSB customers had the advantage of on-line banking. This service is still available, but the TSB has now been joined by other banks. You can access the Internet pages of all of the major banks by clicking on their names. You also have on this page specialised information relating to banking, such as borrowing and saving.

CSi excels at providing up-to-date information, especially in relation to the business community. You can keep track of any investments you may have made, or see how the market is doing before purchasing any stocks or shares for yourself or your company. Click on the Investment entry to access these pages.

You can see instantly where you are in the Community from this status bar.

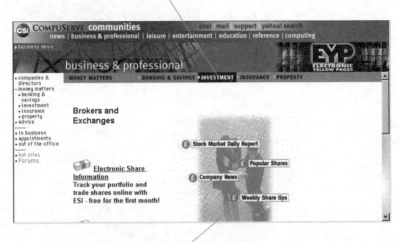

To see the latest share tips, click here.

REMEMBER

You can always move back to a previous page with this button.

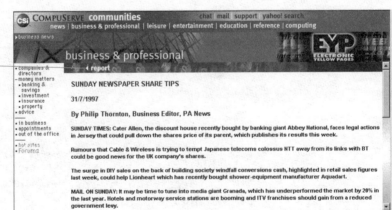

You can also keep track of investments from this Community.

1 Click on the hyperlink (the underlined text) to move to the Electronic Share Information Web page.

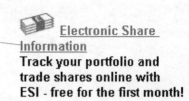

Electronic Share Information
Track your portfolio and trade shares online with ESI - free for the first month!

2 New users should look at the introductory pages. They will also give you an idea of the costs involved with this service.

REMEMBER

Some of these sites do charge for their services, so check before you fill in any electronic forms that you may see on their Web pages.

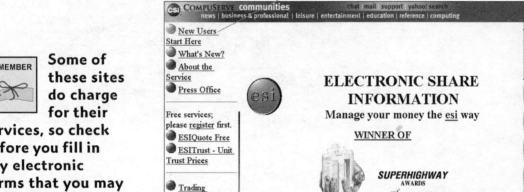

To move back to the Business & Professional start page you will have to click on the button at the top of the page. Viewing Web pages from within your CSi software doesn't give you as much versatility as you could have if Web pages were viewed externally. You have to decide if you would like the maximum versatility when viewing Web pages, or if you would like easy access to the other services from CSi.

Leisure

The Leisure Community covers everything from travel information, including timetables and flight information, to tips on how to improve your garden. Click on the Leisure button now to go to the main screen.

When the page has been fully displayed this logo will animate. Click on any section that interests you to go to that page.

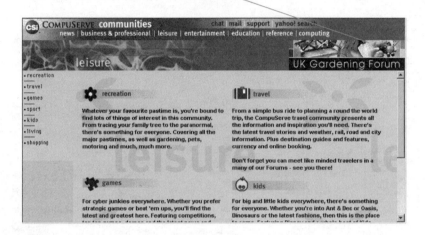

As you can see, each of the entries in the main screen has a corresponding button on the left. You can either click on the text on the left of the screen as you were doing in the last section, or click on the hotspot graphics in the main window. For example:

Click on the Recreation logo on the main screen.

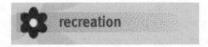

2 This is the main Recreation screen. Notice that a corresponding entry has been put under the Leisure heading to indicate where you are in the Community. You can move back to the first page simply by clicking on the word Leisure.

HANDY TIP

As you move deeper into any of the Communities, it can get a little confusing where you have already visited. If you do get lost, go back to the opening page of the Community to get your bearings before continuing.

Use these hotspots to move to these sections of the Community.

3 Click on the Gardening entry on the left of the screen to bring up another page on this subject.

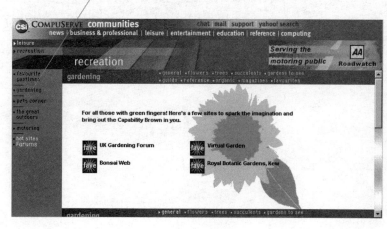

To gain access to Forums related to the Leisure Community, click on the Forums link at the top of the page.

Click on the Forums entry.

If you do enter any of the Forum areas from a Community, then click on the Leave Forum button, you will be taken back to the page from which you originally accessed the Forum.

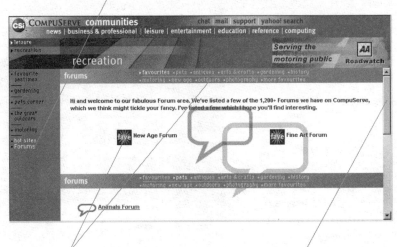

Click on any of these hyperlinks to move to any of the Forums that interest you.

Scroll down the screen to see more Forums.

If you do decide to visit a Forum from a Community, you will see the usual screens open that you saw at the beginning of this chapter. Another area of the Leisure Community that most members find of use is the Travel pages area. If you move back to the first page in the Leisure Community, you will see this logo. Click on it now.

Clicking on the Travel hotspot will open this page.

If you visit this page regularly you can keep
up-to-date with the latest travel news.

Use these specialised pages to
check holiday information.

If you scroll down the page you will see links to some
Forums that might be of interest.

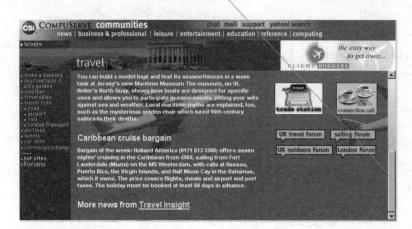

On the Make a Booking page you will see these two graphics. As you can see, the Travel Centre Online offers CSi members discounts on a wide range of holidays. Click on the graphic to go to their Web page.

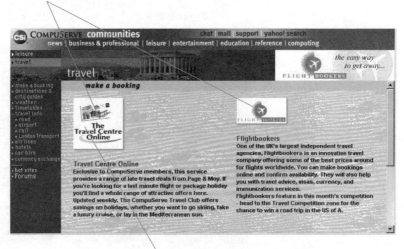

Note that you can always access the other Communities from the main title bar.

This is a standard Web page. All the graphics here are hotspots. Click on them to move to the page that interests you.

On the opening Travel screen you will see an entry for timetables. Clicking on this opens the screen below. As you can see, you have a wide range of timetable information to choose from, including National Express and Eurostar.

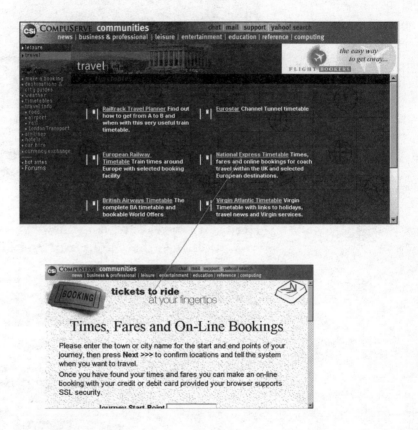

You have the option with some of the timetable information of not only checking on an arrival or departure, but also booking your seats from the comfort of your home. This is possible with the National Express and British Airways Web sites, which you can visit by clicking on the entries on this page.

Entertainment

The Entertainment Community gives you access to information and news on a wide variety of entertainment that you and your family can enjoy as members of CSi.

For instance, among the most popular are the music pages. Here you can read the latest news about the music world. As you can see, there are many hyperlinks to explore.

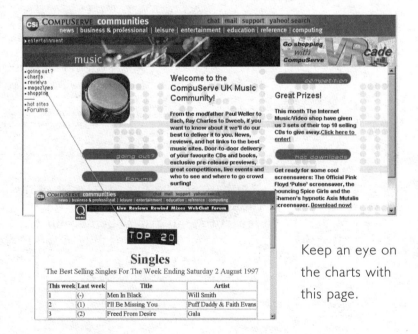

Keep an eye on the charts with this page.

One of the most widely used pages in the Entertainment Community is the Film page. You can read the latest gossip, enter competitions and jump to a large number of other Web sites that any film buff would find interesting.

REMEMBER

Some sites also have corresponding Forum pages. If you look back at page 114 of Chapter Six, you will see that you can access the Forum for the Empire film magazine from that page as well as the one opposite.

The E Drive Web site is an on-line magazine that film fans will want to keep a check on.

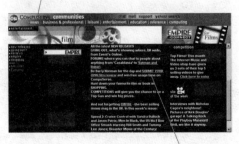

You can also read the latest film news at the Empire site.

At this site, you can send in your own review of a film you have seen, and maybe win some free time on CSi.

Education

Here in the Education Community you can search for information about a university you are interested in. Also, if you have a CSi link at school, you can participate in Global School Link, and talk to other schools across the world.

REMEMBER

Remember that you also have the Reference Community, which offers a huge amount of educational information on its pages. You can see a taste of what is available beginning on page 148.

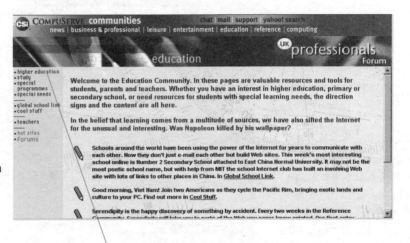

| Click on the Higher Education link on the left of the screen.

2 You will see the Higher Education screen open. Click here to access a clickable map of UK universities.

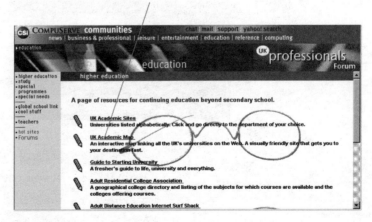

3 Look at the map and choose a university that you would like more information on, then click on its entry. You will be taken to the Web page of the university of your choice.

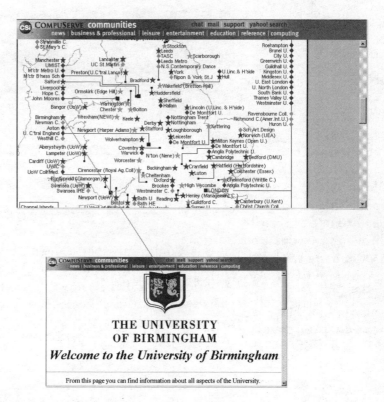

...contd

If you move back to the first page of the Education Community, you will see an entry called Global School Link. Click on this now.

If your school wants to have a go at creating a Web page and then submitting it to CSi, the software that CSi provides can be used. This is very easy to use and will allow you to design a Web page with the least amount of technical knowledge. The next chapter covers this in detail.

In this Community you can communicate with schools across the world that have a link to the Internet. From America to the Far East, you can talk to any school that is registered. As you can see from the first page opposite, you can communicate with a school from China or Japan. Also notice in the first paragraph of this page that you have the chance to get your school onto this page.

This Community really lets you participate in the CSi service, if your school has a home page. This is what is meant when it says 'submit your URL'. If your page is good enough, CSi may feature it on this page. If you don't have any home page creation software, don't worry. In the next chapter you will learn how to get hold of CSi's own home page designing software. This is a very quick and easy way to create a home page. All you need is to add your own imagination.

To see a school's home page, click on the SchoolNet UK link.

To see a school's home page, click on the SchoolNet UK link.

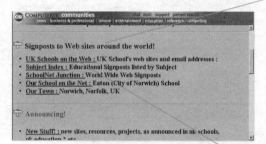

If you scroll down this screen, you will see other schools listed that have their own Web pages.

Again, use the scroll bars to find a school's home page that interests you.

Reference

One of the most useful aspects of the whole CSi service is the amount of reference information that you have access to as a member. You have already seen that you have access to a wide range of timetable information in the Travel Community. In the Reference Community you have even more information available with a few clicks of the mouse.

The Community opens with the on-line encyclopedia, which you can search for any information that you can think of. You may have seen this encyclopedia on CD-ROM as a stand-alone title. CSi now provides this store of knowledge on-line through this community. To use this encyclopedia follow these steps.

HANDY TIP

Before you use the search engine on the encyclopedia, it's a good idea to read through the text below it, as this gives you detailed information on how this part of the encyclopedia works.

As you can see from this screenshot, this page looks very much like an Internet search engine such as Yahoo! or Infoseek. You enter your request for information and then ask the software to search its database for anything that matches your query. Input your query in this box, then click the Search button.

...contd

REMEMBER

Any entry that is underlined in the encyclopedia will take you to another page. This is just like a hyperlink on an ordinary Internet Web page.

2 Click on any of the entries that have been found to jump straight to the relevant page in the encyclopedia.

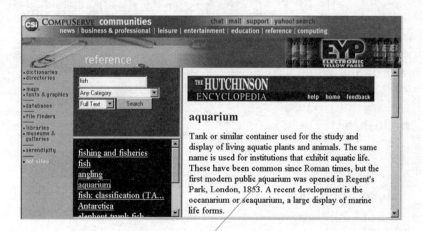

3 You can now read what information the encyclopedia has on your chosen topic in the main window on the right of the screen.

If you are having problems finding what you are looking for, you can narrow your search parameters. What this means is that you type in a phrase that is closer to the information that you are looking for. The encyclopedia's help screen explains how to do this. Instead of just searching all of the encyclopedia, you can choose a specific category to search in.

Click on the down arrow on the main page and you will see this menu open.

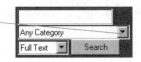

The skills that you learn here when you are entering search phrases will come in very handy when you try and search for information on the Internet. The Internet is vast, whereas the encyclopedia is enclosed, and only has a certain amount of information on offer.

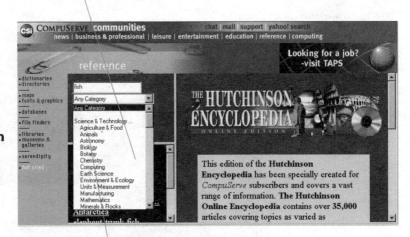

2 Click on a category that you think your search query falls into.

The encyclopedia will now have a better idea of the kind of information you are looking for when you enter your text and then click the Search button.

This community offers other dictionaries as well as the Hutchinson encyclopedia. If you click on the Dictionaries link on the left of the page, you will see this screen open. As you can see, you have a wide selection to choose from. You should be able to find some information on just about any subject.

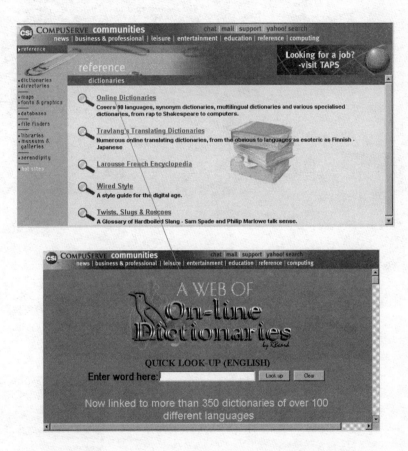

Click on any of the dictionaries on this page. You will be taken to their home pages where you can search their databases for the information you are looking for. If you scroll down the English dictionary screen, you will be able to choose from dozens of dictionaries in other languages that you can search in the same way as you would the English dictionary. You also have access to other dictionaries from this page.

Directories

Not to be confused with dictionaries, CSi also has a comprehensive list of directories that you can access in the same way that you used the encyclopedia section of this Community.

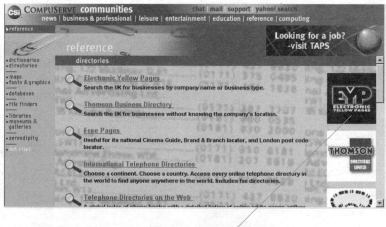

Use this search engine in the same way as you use the encyclopedia's search engine.

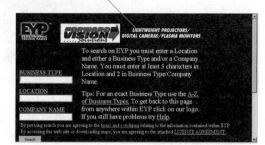

...contd

Another very useful source of information is the Which? Directory. If you go back to the main Directories screen and scroll down it, you will see the Which? entry.

You don't have to worry about missing an issue of any of the magazines that you can search on-line, as they are always available to you. Also, if you want to search a magazine for features in a back issue that you don't have, this is also possible. More and more magazines are providing this information on-line. The vast majority of it is also free!

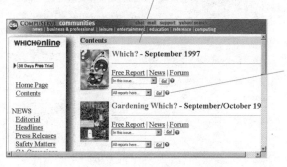

Search for the latest information in each issue of the magazine.

Use the drop-down menus to help you search in the correct areas.

Databases

The whole Internet has been likened to a vast database of information that you can search from the comfort of your own home. CSi offers easy access to a number of on-line databases that you can easily search for any topic that interests you.

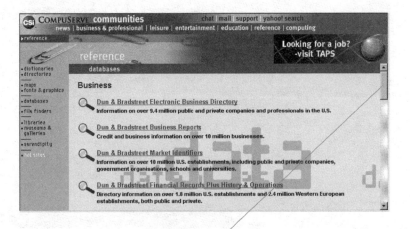

As an example of the databases available, scroll down the screen above and click on the drug databases entry.

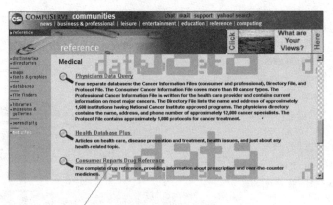

2 Click on the Drug Reference link.

3 You will see this dialogue box open. Click on the Proceed button.

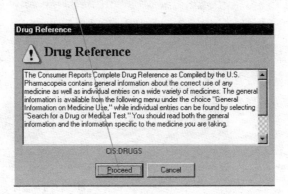

4 Enter a drug name that you would like to search for information on and click OK.

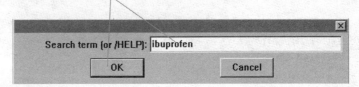

5 This page will show you what brand names the drug is known by. You can also see information on how to use the drug safely and what possible side-effects you may encounter.

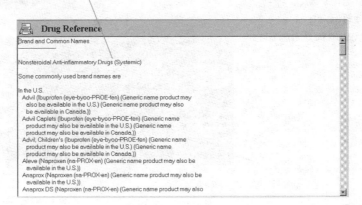

Museums & Galleries

If you are planning a visit to one of the great museums in London, this area of the Reference Community will be of great help. Most of the large museums now have Web sites. You can plan your visit and even see some of the exhibitions on-line if you can't visit the museum in person. Also, they have a great deal of information that compliments the other reference areas of this Community.

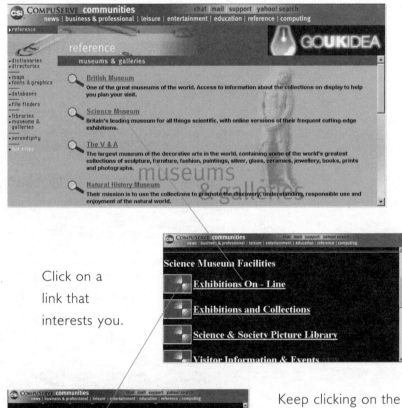

HANDY TIP

You can use this Community in relation with the Travel Community, with its timetable database, to plan your entire visit to any of the museums and galleries that are represented here.

Click on a link that interests you.

Keep clicking on the links as they appear to see more and more detail on the exhibition that you are interested in.

...contd

If you scroll down the first page of the Museums and Galleries section, you will see this area of the page. Here you can see real-time movies that illustrate some of the exhibitions on offer. You will need special software to view these movies on your computer, but you can also see that there are two buttons on the page. These are hyperlinks to the Web sites of the companies that will allow you to download the software you need to view these movies. A lot of the museum sites are now interactive. Don't be afraid to click on the links you see. You may be surprised at what you find on these sites.

Click on any of these links to
see real-time movies about
the museum's exhibitions.

If you have a slow Internet connection, movies can take a long time to download. If you have a modem that is running at less than 28,800 bps, now is the time to upgrade.

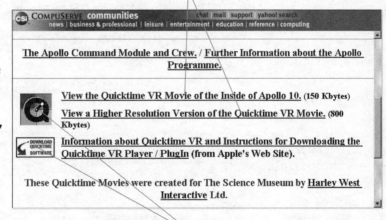

Use these links to download the software
you need to view the movies on offer.

...contd

One of the world's most outstanding museums is the Natural History Museum in London. Their entry in the Reference Community allows you to view their extensive site, check out the new exhibitions and plan your visit. If you have been to the museum before, you will know that there is a lot to take in. These pages have full floorplans of the whole museum so you can plan where you want to go before you travel to the museum itself, saving you a great deal of time.

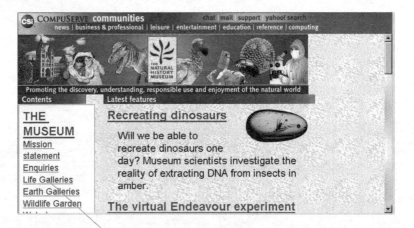

Some sites are virtually impossible to make sense of in non-graphics mode. It is always much better to leave the graphics switched on unless you have a very slow Internet connection.

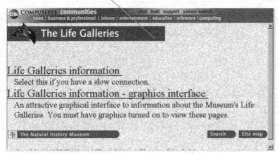

Clicking on the Life Galleries entry on the main page will open this area of the site. Here you have a choice of how you view the rest of this site, depending on the speed of your connection. Viewing this site in graphics mode is essential, so if you have a slower modem here's the excuse you needed to upgrade. Click on the graphics interface entry to move to the next screen.

...contd

You can also view the floorplans of the museum from this page if you want to see where the subject you have just chosen is located in the building.

HANDY TIP

As you plan your visit, you can print out the floorplans that you need and take them with you.

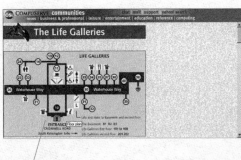

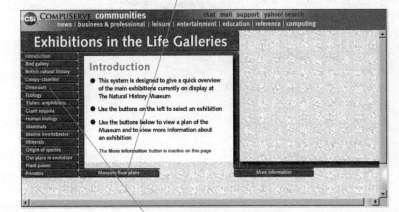

Click on any of the buttons to see information about that subject.

When accessing any Web site that is as large as the Natural History Museum's, you can have problems finding your way about the site as you look for information or plan your visit. A lot of Web sites these days have site maps that show you how the pages are linked together. The Natural History Museum site has a site map that is easy to understand, and therefore allows you to get the most from the site when you visit it. You can see this page from the first page you saw when you entered the museum's site, or you can click on the Site Map button that you see on the Life Galleries page.

HANDY TIP

Whenever you visit a large Internet site, look for a site map. They can be a very useful way of getting an idea of how the site is laid out, and where you can find the information you are looking for.

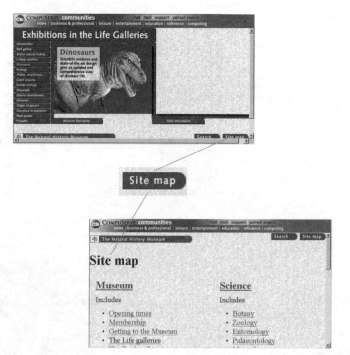

All these entries are hyperlinks like those you have seen throughout the new CSi Communities. Scroll down the screen until you see something of interest, then click on the entry. You will then move straight to that page on the museum's Web site.

As CSi is a global network, you are not limited to those museums based in the UK. If you scroll down the main screen you will see a link that will allow you to access museums and galleries from all over the world.

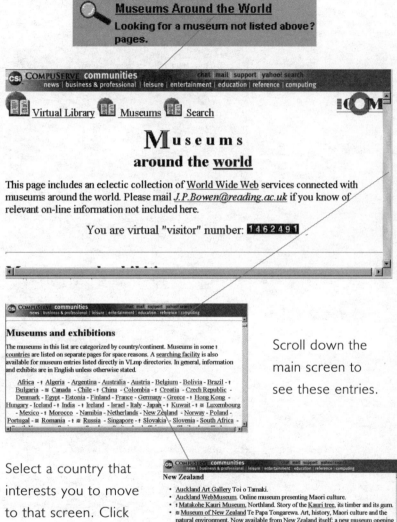

Scroll down the main screen to see these entries.

Select a country that interests you to move to that screen. Click on a museum or gallery to move to its Web site.

Computing

Catch up on the latest computing news and read reviews of the latest software and hardware in this Community. The large buttons in the main window are the major computing news items at the moment. Click on the arrow to read the news item. You will see your mouse pointer change to a pointing hand when you are over a link that will take you to another page.

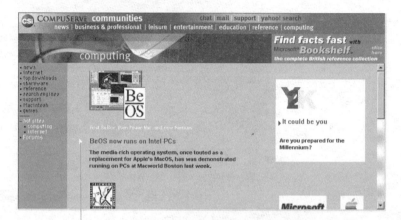

Click here to see CSi's news coverage of this story.

Click on hyperlinks like this to move to related pages.

...contd

You can get more specific news on particular topics by clicking on the News entry on the left of the main screen.

Click on this entry to see the News screen.

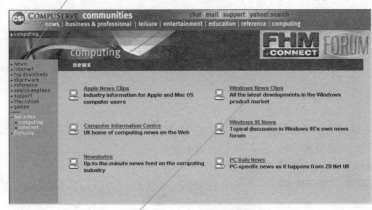

REMEMBER **You will also find technology news in the main News Community.**

Click on any of the entries on this page to see specific news. They are very much like the support Forums that many companies have on the CSi service to help their customers.

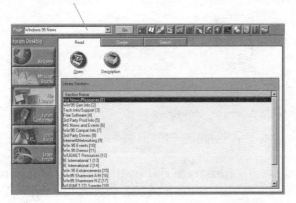

From the main News screen you also have access to the ZD Net Web site. This is the Web site of the publishers Ziff-Davies. Their site is packed with computing news and reviews of the latest hardware and software, as well as links to other sites that you might find useful. This is an excellent site that you should try to visit at regular intervals.

PC Daily News
PC-specific news as it happens from ZD Net UK

HANDY TIP

There is a lot to take in on sites like this. Make a point each time you log on to go to this Web site and look at a little more of it. This way you won't use up your valuable on-line time with just one site.

These are links even though they are not underlined. They offer more specialised information.

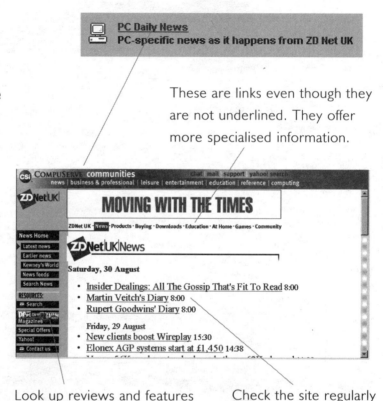

Look up reviews and features in Ziff-Davies magazines.

Check the site regularly for the latest news.

To illustrate the usefulness of this site, click on the Products link at the top of the page. You will be taken to another set of pages that allow you to check up on new products and reviews before you decide which model of hardware or software to buy.

Detailed product reviews of the latest hardware and software can be read here.

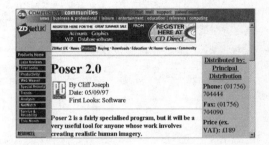

This is a very informal section of the ZD Net site. Here you can take part in the Community that forms a focus for the site.

Internet

This is the page to go to if you are new to the Internet, or if you want to search for some specific information about the Web. You can get advice, download help files and get hold of the latest software to make accessing the Web easier and quicker.

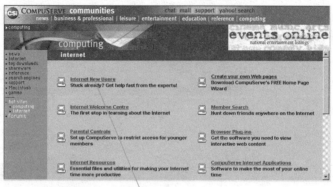

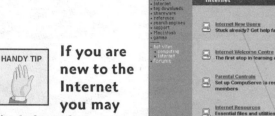

HANDY TIP

If you are new to the Internet you may find that there are a large number of files that you want to download. Try and choose a time when the system isn't too busy, and download the files in one session. You will then be able to refer to multiple files as you need to. Otherwise you will have to keep reconnecting to download another file you find you need to compliment the one you are reading.

Click on this hyperlink to go to the very useful Internet Forum page. Here you will find files that you can download which explain in easy-to-follow instructions how to set your modem up, use FTP (File Transfer Protocol) and access Usenet to name but a few. Click on the file that interests you and you will see the usual Window Save window open. Choose a location that you would like the file to be saved to and then click OK. The file will now be transferred to your hard drive. You can then log off and read this at your leisure.

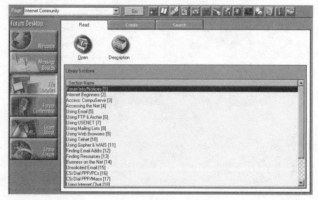

Search Engines

Search engines allow you to search the Internet for information on any subject you can possibly imagine. CSi members have easy access to all the major search engines that are available at the moment. Click on a link in the main window below to move to the search engine's home page. You will then be able to enter your request. Most of the search engines are based in the US, so you will get a large number of US-oriented sites listed. There are some UK-specific engines, like the one shown below, which lists only those sites that are based in the UK and Ireland.

HANDY TIP

Not all search engines operate in the same way. Read the help files so you compose a search phrase that the particular search engine you are using will make the most of. This way you will see the most useful Web sites listed.

Click here in the Computing Community to access the Yahoo UK & Ireland search engine.

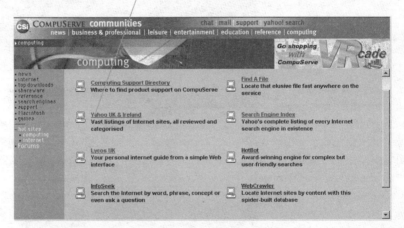

Enter the search words in this box and then click OK to receive a list of hyperlinks matching your query.

Support

Most of the major software and hardware manufacturers have a presence on CSi. Through the Support area they keep in contact with their customers with news of new products and with technical support. If you find you have a problem, you may find an answer here.

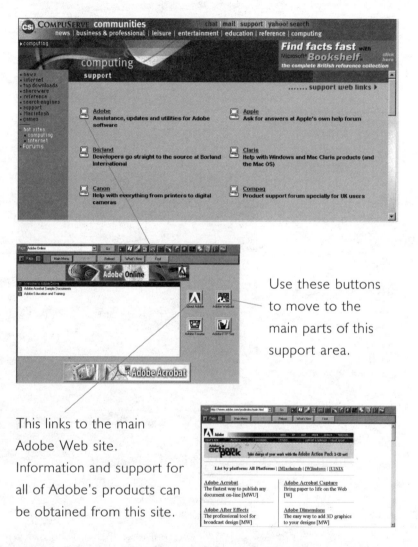

Use these buttons to move to the main parts of this support area.

This links to the main Adobe Web site. Information and support for all of Adobe's products can be obtained from this site.

Most of the support sites appear just like Forums in their layout and access. They also sometimes give you direct access to a company's main Web page, as here with the Adobe support page.

...contd

You also have a link on this page to the major companies' web sites. On the top left of the main screen is the Support Web Links button. Click on this now to go to the main access page.

.... support web links ▶

Note that you can move back to the main CSi service with this button.

REMEMBER

The vast majority of companies' Web sites are best viewed with a full Internet browser. If you still have the CSi software set so the browser is running internally, it is a good idea to switch this to external running before you access any major Web sites. You will find navigation of these sites much easier if you are using a full browser.

Access all these major companies by clicking on their names.

Once you have moved to any of the companies' Web sites, you can see the latest news on products and also download the new beta versions of programs you are thinking of buying.

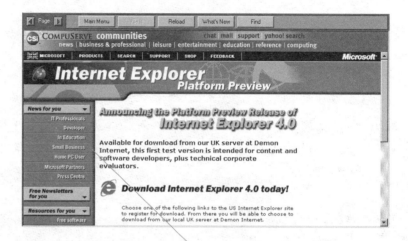

These buttons are all hyperlinks. Click on any that interests you to move to that page on the Web site.

This chapter has given you a tour of the new Communities that CompuServe has created. You can access these at any time and keep up-to-date with the latest news from around the world, or play games on-line, or even do some shopping. At the front of this book you will see a quick reference page. Here all of the main topics that each Community has in it are listed. If you are not sure where to look for some specific information, or can't remember which Community a heading comes under, this page should help you.

Parental Controls

While CSi has many Forums and Communities that any business would find useful, CSi's other role is in the home, as an information source. Parents who have a PC connected to the Internet via CSi may be concerned that their children will come into contact with unsuitable material. Children may simply come across an unsuitable Web site when they are searching for perfectly innocent information.

To help with this problem – but at the same time trying not to limit access or condone censorship – CSi has a number of features that parents can use to limit the material that their children can access via CSi. Click on the Parents Controls to go to the screen you see below.

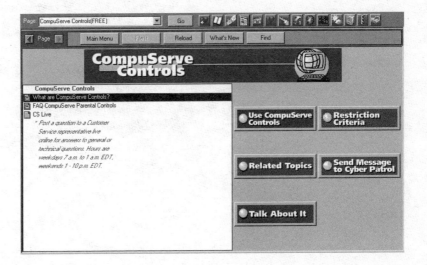

As you can see from the buttons on the right of the screen, you have a great deal of control over the content that your children can access. You can also join a Forum that specialises in this subject. For now we will look at how you can easily limit the access that your children have to the CSi service.

Click on the Use CompuServe Controls button.

2 You have to choose a password to gain access to these control settings. Choose one that is personal to you. Confirm it and then click OK.

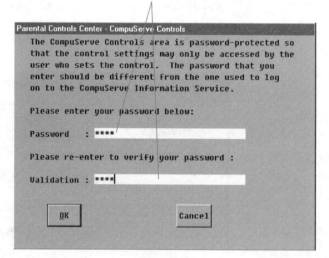

3 If you ever forget your password, you don't have to set all your settings again – you can choose another password. To allow you to do this easily in the future, CSi now asks you to enter a question and answer. If you forget your password, CSi will ask you the question you entered. If you can provide the correct answer, your identity will be confirmed and you will be allowed to continue to use your previously-entered settings.

...contd

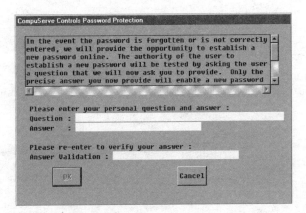

4 The last dialogue box you will see allows you to set what kind of restricted access you want. This can either be to the CSi service itself, or to the Internet. You can also choose if the limited access is for this session only or permanent. Choose your settings and then click the Permanent or Session Only button to complete the setup.

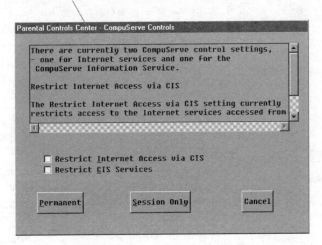

5 When you have decided that the access limits you have set are correct, you will see the following dialogue box to allow you to confirm all of the settings. If you are happy with what you have set, click OK. Access will now be limited.

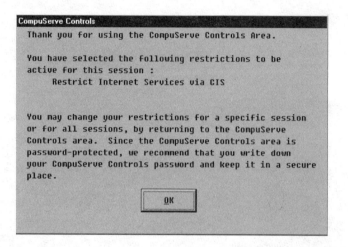

If you have any questions about Parental Controls, you can access the FAQs (Frequently Asked Questions) page. If you still don't find the answer to your question, you can ask a CSi customer services representative, who should be able to help you.

Your Personal Home Page

As part of your membership to CompuServe you have some free space on the service for you to store your own home page. CSi also provides software that allows you to quickly and easily create your home page and publish it on the Internet for others to visit.

Covers

Chapter Eight

Our World

Our World is an area of the CSi service where you can gain access to files and help with building your own home page, which you can then publish on the Internet, using the free space on the CSi servers that is made available as part of your membership. CSi make the creation of this home page straightforward, using a Wizard. You will most likely have seen Wizards at work already.

To access the Our World area of the CSi service and download the Home Page Wizard, you should follow these steps.

Remember, most of the CSi service has a Go command. You can move very quickly to a Forum or Community area if you know its Go address.

The easiest way to move to the Our World area of CSi is to use the Go command. Click on the Go button and you will see this dialogue box open. Enter 'ourworld', then click OK.

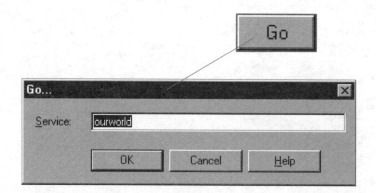

2 Opposite you can see the main Our World screen. From here you can download the software you need, go to the Our World Web page, or join some of the Forums that are available to help you with your own home page.

...contd

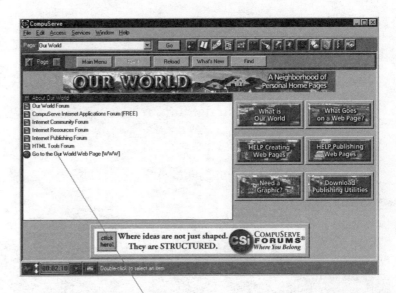

3 Double-click on the 'Go to the Our World Web Page' link.

4 You will now move to the Our World Web page, as you see below. Click on the 'Publish in Our World' button.

REMEMBER

You can access this Web site if you have set your Internet Preferences to use your browser internally as well as externally, as you see here.

5 This is the area of the Our World Web page where you can download the Home Page and Publishing Wizards.

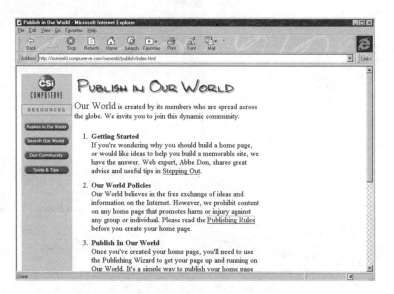

The file you are downloading is compressed or 'zipped' to a smaller size than it normally is. You will be extracting it later so that you can run the program. The Home Page Wizard and the Publishing Wizard are together less than a megabyte in size. Make sure the drive that you extract the files to has enough free space on it.

6 Scroll down the page, then click on the 'Download the Home Page and Publishing Wizards now' link.

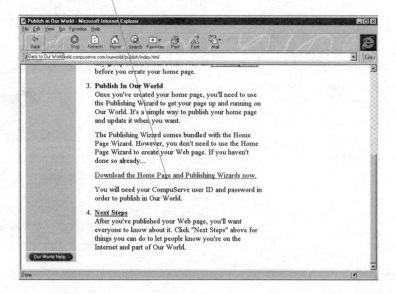

...contd

When the file is down- loaded, take notice of where the file has been saved, especially if you have not used the default save which puts the file in the cserv folder on your 'C' drive. You will need to locate this later to extract the software

7 You will now see that you are on the Author Tools page of the Our World Web site. If you now click on the 'Get it now' entry as you see here, the Home Page Wizard will be transferred to your computer.

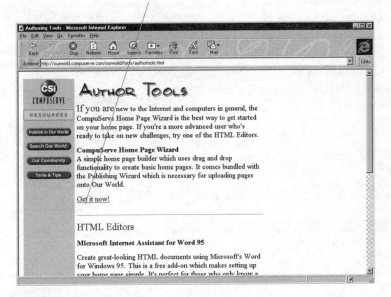

8 When the file hpwiz.exe has downloaded, you should see this icon in the folder you selected to download to.

Double-click on the icon. You will see this dialogue box to confirm that you have the software. Click OK to move to the next dialogue box.

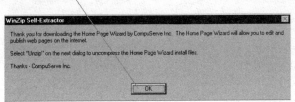

...contd

REMEMBER

The directory that is shown here can be changed to any one that you choose. This is just the Windows default that is used each time a file is downloaded.

9 This dialogue box will open. From here you extract the software so that you can use it on your computer. Click on the Unzip button to continue.

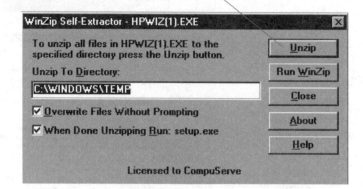

10 When you begin to extract the files, you will see the standard setup Wizard, the first screen of which you can see below.

When the setup Wizard has finished you will see all of the Home Page Wizard files appear in the Hpwiz folder, which in turn should be in the Cserv folder on your hard drive – unless you chose a different location in step 9.

11 Double-click on the Hpwiz icon in the folder to start the Home Page Wizard.

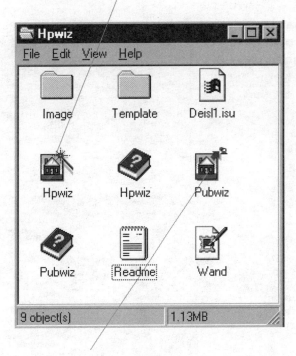

This is the program you will use later to publish your newly-designed home page onto the CSi Web server for other people to visit.

You have now successfully downloaded the Home Page Wizard software and installed it on your computer. The next topic will show you how to use the Wizard to create a basic home page that you can publish on the Internet.

The Home Page Wizard

| Double-click on this icon, which you saw in step 11 of the previous section, to start the Home Page Wizard.

Hpwiz

2 This is the first screen of the Home Page Wizard. Enter a title for your home page and a project name, then click the Next button.

Note that the project name can only be 8 characters long.

3 Enter your personal information in this form and then click on the Next button to move to the next screen.

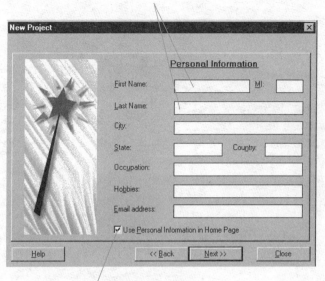

Tick this box if you want your personal information to appear on your home page.

4 The next screen allows you to choose how your home page will look. Select a style, then click Next.

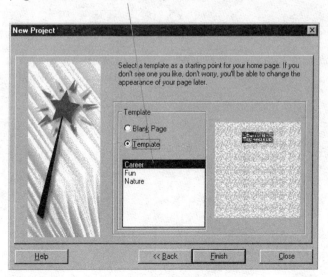

5 Click finish when you are happy with the look of your home page. It will now be opened so you can edit it.

 Try not to use large graphics on your page, as they take up a great deal of memory and take a long time to download.

You can now customise the design of your new home page, adding text and graphics. The program allows you to modify all the elements that go up to make a Web page. Its functions are accessed through the icons at the top of the screen, and are quite straightforward. However, to learn about any of the functions, you can refer to the on-line help by clicking on the Help icon at the right of the screen.

Finally, as you saw in step 2 on page 176, you can always join one of the Our World Forums if you have a question you would like to ask. There is bound to be another member who can help you.

The Publishing Wizard

Once you have created your home page you will no doubt want to move it to the World-Wide Web as soon as possible so that others can see it. CSi makes this a very easy task, using the Publishing Wizard, which you downloaded along with the Home Page Wizard. The Publishing Wizard takes all the files that make up your homepage, and transfers them to the CSi server.

When you down-loaded the Home Page Wizard and Publishing Wizard, you had a chance to change the default path that these programs were saved to. If you did this, go to the folder you saved them in.

1   Open the folder on your hard drive that contains all of your CompuServe files. This is usually on drive 'C' in the folder labelled 'CSERV'.

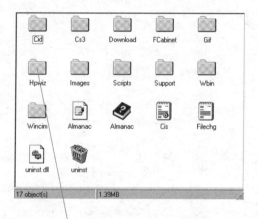

2   Open the folder Hpwiz. Locate the program file Pubwiz, then double-click on it.

Pubwiz

3   This is the opening screen of the Publishing Wizard. Click Next to move to the next screen.

4 Use this dialogue box to decide if you want to upload a new set of pages, or delete an existing set. Click Next when you have made your choice.

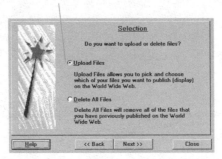

5 You must enter this personal information in this dialogue box. This is used by CompuServe as your entry in the CompuServe Home Page Directory.

6 You have the option of leaving this dialogue box blank. This information is used by CSi when a user searches the directory for other users with a particular hobby or occupation.

...contd

Try and group all the files that you need to upload in the same folder. This will allow you to select them easily in the upload dialogue box.

7 This message box precedes the main upload dialogue box. Click on Next to move to the file-selection screen.

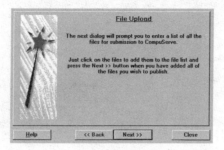

8 This dialogue box allows you to select all the graphic files and text files that make up your home page. Select a file and click on Add to enter it in the upload window.

The two most common graphic formats in use on the Web are GIF and JPEG. These both use data compression to make the files as small as possible.

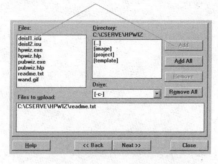

9 In this dialogue box you can select which file will be displayed first when someone accesses your home page. This is usually the welcome screen, but you can specify any page you like.

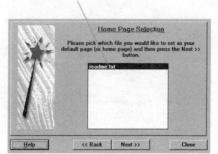

...contd

10 Enter your user ID and password here. You must have a valid account with CSi before you can upload your home page files. You will also see this dialogue box if you are using the Publishing Wizard to delete some files from the CSi server.

 If your home page is too large for the free space that you are given as part of your CSi membership, you can lease more space from CSi, but this will cost you more money each month.

11 You have now entered all the information that the Wizard needs to publish your home page. If you want to check

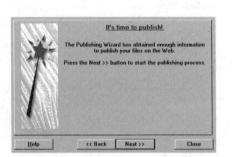

any of the details, click on the Back button now. If not, click Next.

12 This is your final chance to cancel the publishing operation. After you click the Proceed button, you will see a disclaimer from CompuServe and then your pages will be uploaded.

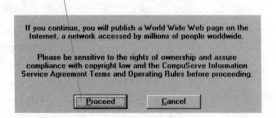

Index